Preschool ABC Bible Heroes

by Marcia Noel Hornok

illustrated by Shelly Rasche

Cover by Jeff Van Kanegan

Shining Star Publications, Copyright © 1993

ISBN No. 0-86653-697-3

Standardized Subject code TA ac

Printing No. 98765432

Shining Star Publications
1204 Buchanan St., Box 299
Carthage, IL 62321-0299

The purchase of this book entitles the buyer to reproduce student activity pages for classroom use only. Any other use requires written permission from Shining Star Publications.

All rights reserved. Printed in the United States of America.

Unless otherwise indicated, the New International Version of the Bible was used in preparing the activities in this book.

Dedication

To the anonymous teacher
who showed this five-year-old her need to have
Jesus as Savior.

To Pastor Glenn F. Yeckley,
who taught her what it meant to follow
Jesus as Shepherd.

To Paul Q. Noel,
Daddy, who still nurtures her desire to know
Jesus as Sovereign.

To the Teacher/Parent

A child's first classroom experiences must be enjoyable, or his academic career may be jeopardized. Passive learning (involving eyes and ears) is not enough to stimulate preschool children to learn. These little ones must also feel, do, taste, move, sing, and play.

This book offers simple songs, rhymes, games, whole-body activities, pretending exercises, and easy crafts. Eleven chapters feature Bible personalities and songs about their lives. The easy songs have repetitive words set to familiar tunes (no new melodies to practice).

Phonics skills; "let's pretend" games emphasizing participation, not competition; and action exercises are suited to the preschool child's physical and mental abilities. Children will be challenged to learn new skills and concepts through enjoyable experiences.

A page for the child to color and keep in his own ABC book will reinforce the letters and colors he is learning. Chapters culminate with a rhyming mini book for the child to take home and use as a review.

Through these creative methods children will learn alphabet recognition and sounds, colors, and numbers one through twelve as they study famous Bible people.

Whether using this book at home, in Sunday School classes, children's church, or Christian schools, your children will learn by doing. They will grow in Christian character, academic skills, physical coordination, and creativity, while having fun.

If you will be using this book in a classroom setting, you will need the following items:
> folder or slim binder for each student (p. 6); blue ribbons or cloth strips, beanbags for half the class (p. 11); purple sock (p. 16); large buttons (pp. 11, 68); medium grocery sacks (p. 18); plastic eggs from hosiery (p. 25); four green lids (p. 32); 6-oz. juice cans (p. 35); cardboard tubes (p. 41); gift boxes and shoe boxes (p. 42); dice (pp. 48, 91); spools of colored thread (p. 78); lids from gallon jugs, various colors if possible (p. 80); egg cartons (p. 91).

Table of Contents

Chapter 1 6
- *A* — Adam
- *B* — Bible
- Color — Blue
- Number — One

Chapter 2 14
- *C* — Clothes
- *D* — Dorcas
- Color — Purple
- Number — Two

Chapter 3 22
- *E* — Elijah
- *F* — Food
- Color — Orange
- Number — Three

Chapter 4 30
- *G* — Gift
- *H* — Hannah
- Color — Green
- Number — Four

Chapter 5 37
- *I* — Israel
- *J* — Joshua
- Color — Grey
- Number — Five

Chapter 6 45
- *K* — King
- *L* — Lamb
- Color — Brown
- Number — Six

Chapter 7 53
M – Mary
N – Night
Color – Black
Number – Seven

Chapter 8 60
O – Oval
P – Peter
Color – Pink
Number – Eight

Chapter 9 68
Q – Queen
R – Red
Color – Red
Number – Review

Chapter 10 75
S – Samson
T – Ten
Color – Review
Number – Ten

Chapter 11 82
U – Us
V – Vowels
W – White
Color – White
Number – Eleven

Chapter 12 89
X – eXercise
Y – Yellow
Z – Zacchaeus
Color – Yellow
Number – Twelve

Chapter 1

***A* is for Adam.** *B* **is for Bible.**

Note to teacher:
Each child should have his own copy of the alphabet–association pictures in each chapter. Keep them in a folder or binder after the child colors them.

Children should make the frame the color emphasized for that chapter. At the end of the series, they will have their own ABC books for review.

Also post alphabet sheets in the room as letters are learned. Each day review the colors and the letters in unison:

A is for Adam. (Teacher makes the sound of the letter *A* as in Adam.) *B* is for Bible. (Teacher makes the sound of the letter *B* as in Bible.)

When the children are ready, a distinction can be made between the name of the letter (*A,B*) and its sound.

Learning the sound of the letter is an important prereading phonics skill.

Did You Ever?
Tune: "Did You Ever See a Lassie?"

Did you ever read the Bible, the Bible, the Bible?
Did you ever read the Bible?
It's God's Word to me.

Did you ever hear of Adam, of Adam, of Adam?
Did you ever hear of Adam?
The first man God made.

You can read it in the Bible, the Bible, the Bible.
You can read it in the Bible.
It's God's Word to me.

Substitute other names for "Adam" in the second stanza, especially as subsequent chapters are taught.

Children will enjoy singing the above song while standing in a circle, holding hands, and walking. On each stanza, reverse directions.

A is for Adam and Animal.

B is for Bible.

Color the frame blue.

Color Fun: Blue

Show children which crayon or marker is blue. Instruct them to color the frame around their alphabet picture blue. Review the sound of the letter *B*.

Ask every child who is wearing something blue to stand and show it to the class. Acknowledge it by saying "Timmy's shirt has blue on it, Amber's socks are blue," etc.

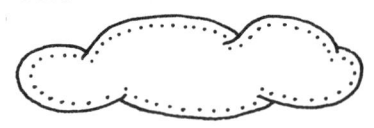

Finger Play: Blue Things

Blue, blue, the *skies* are blue.	*(Wave hands gently overhead.)*
Blink, blink, some *eyes* are blue.	*(Hold hands near eyes; open and close fingers.)*
Splish, splash, the *lakes* are blue.	*(Swing hands side to side imitating waves.)*
Yummy, yummy, some *cakes* are blue.	*(Rub "tummy" in circular motion with one hand.)*

Tune: "Twinkle, Twinkle, Little Star"

Blue is-the color of the skies.
Blue is-the color of some eyes.
Blue is-the color of the lakes
And some happy birthday cakes.
Yes, I like the color blue.
Do-o you-ou like blue, too?

(Older children can talk about the words that rhyme in the last sentence.)

You may want to have a "Blue Day" with everyone wearing or bringing something blue. For treats, enjoy blue Popsicles™ or blueberries.

Number Fun: One

One man	*(Hold up index finger on one hand.)*
And one woman.	*(Hold up middle finger on same hand.)*
One tree not to touch!	*(Hold up index finger on other hand.)*
One day they gave in.	*(Touch "man and woman" fingers to "tree" finger on other hand.)*
It was one sin too much.	*(Drop "man and woman" hand. Continue holding up index finger on other hand.)*

Phonics Skill

The letter *A* has several sounds, especially because it's a vowel. To teach the vowel sounds for *A*, repeat this exercise, accenting the bold letters:

A man named **A**dam did something **aw**ful! *(Shake head no.)*

Ate the fruit God told him not to. *(Pretend eating from hand.)*

Uh, Aah, Aw, poor **Aah-Aah-A**dam. *(Shake index finger.)*

God forg**a-a-a**ve his sin. *(Smile and wave hands parallel to floor, palms down.)*

Body Coordination Exercise: The Bible

(Sitting)

The Bible is the book to know. *(Hold hands open like a book.)*

B-I-B-L-E *(Clap on each letter.)*

The Bible is the way to grow. *(Rise from chair.)*

B-I-B-L-E *(Clap on each letter.)*

It is difficult for young children to clap on each letter of B-I-B-L-E. Because this kind of coordination is important to their mental development, have them keep practicing.

Other Suggested Songs:

"The B-I-B-L-E"
"Wordless Book Song"
"I Believe the Bible"
"Read Your Bible, Pray Every Day"
(Tune: "I Will Make You Fishers of Men")

Let's Pretend: Adam's Jobs
(Genesis 2:7-15, 19-20)

After God made Adam, He put him in a beautiful garden. He told Adam to take care of the garden. Let's pretend we are taking care of a garden like Adam did.

What are some things we must do to a garden so that flowers, plants, and trees will grow?

[Everyone can imitate the leader by pretending to shovel dirt, dig, plant seeds, water, cultivate, pull weeds, prune, pick and eat, or whatever the children suggest. (Genesis 2:15)]

God gave Adam another job–naming the animals God had made. God made each animal walk by Adam, and he gave it a name. Let's pretend we are some animals God made, and we're walking to Adam so he can name us. (Genesis 2:19-20)

[Lead the class to imitate characteristics of certain common animals. Then ask "What would Adam name us?" See the following examples.]

Let's pretend we have wings and can fly (flap arms and move around the room) and we say "Tweet, tweet" and eat worms. What would Adam name us?

Let's pretend we hop like this (imitate rabbit hopping), and we have long ears (hold hands up for ears), and we like to eat carrots. What would Adam name us?

Games
Balls, Baskets, Beanbags

1. Side Basketball–Turn a wastebasket on its side. Sit on the floor and try to roll a ball into it. Let each child keep trying until he makes it, moving the basket closer if necessary.

2. Hit the Basket–Show children how to throw a beanbag into an upright wastebasket. If the child is very young, the leader can hold the child's wrist and help with the throwing motion. Give each child three beanbags and see how many she can get into the basket.

3. Ball Roll–Children sit on the floor across from each other or in a circle. They extend their legs in a "V" formation. They take turns rolling a ball into another child's open legs. If children enjoy this, they may want to roll more than one ball at a time.

4. Beanbag Scramble–Divide the class into two teams. Tie a blue ribbon around the upper arm of everyone on one of the teams.

   Put several beanbags (the more, the better) in the center of a designated circle. Children stand around the circle; they must not step over the line until the signal is given.

   At the signal, all children scramble for the beanbags and then return outside the circle. Count how many each team got.

   Repeat several times. This is a team effort. Children can get more than one beanbag or none at all. Encourage them to keep trying.

5. Beanbag Balance–Have each child walk around a circle or from one designated spot to another while balancing a beanbag on his head. Older children may want to have relay races doing this.

6. Whole-Body Exercise–Make motions of using a ball as you repeat this poem:

   Bounce a ball; bounce a ball. Bounce. Bounce. Bounce. Roll a ball; roll a ball. Roll. Roll. Roll. Catch a ball; catch a ball. Catch. Catch. Catch. Throw a ball; throw a ball. Throw. Throw. Throw.

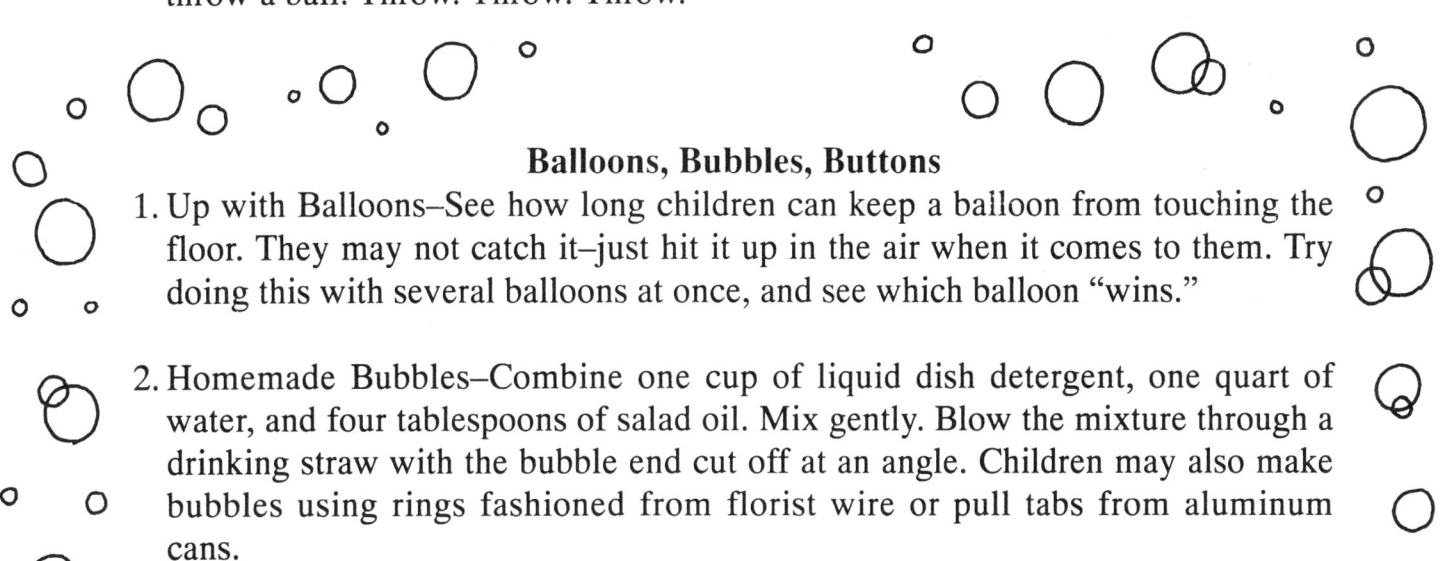

Balloons, Bubbles, Buttons

1. Up with Balloons–See how long children can keep a balloon from touching the floor. They may not catch it–just hit it up in the air when it comes to them. Try doing this with several balloons at once, and see which balloon "wins."

2. Homemade Bubbles–Combine one cup of liquid dish detergent, one quart of water, and four tablespoons of salad oil. Mix gently. Blow the mixture through a drinking straw with the bubble end cut off at an angle. Children may also make bubbles using rings fashioned from florist wire or pull tabs from aluminum cans.

3. Button Toss–Cut one side from a box without a lid. Draw a "target" on the floor of the box or insert one made of poster board. Place the box at one end of a table. Children stand at the other end and throw buttons (the largest you can find) on the target. Older children can learn to play Tiddly Buttons by striking the edge of a button with another button to make it jump.

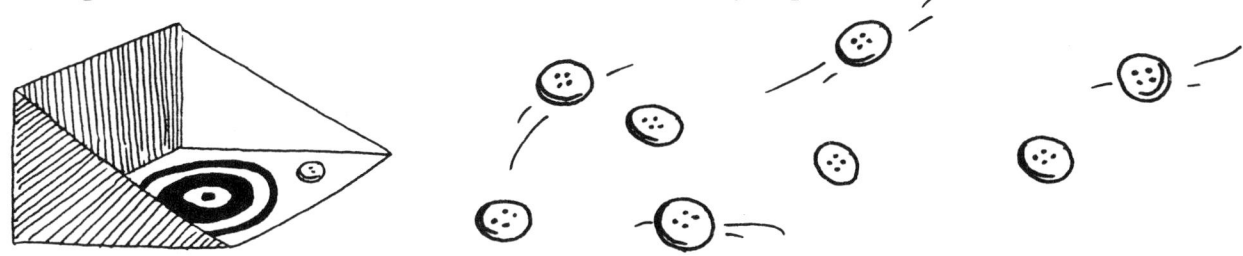

4. Button Race–For two to six children on stairs.

Children sit on the bottom step. A person with a button (button person) stands facing them; he puts his hands behind his back and brings them out with closed fists.

Each seated child tries to guess which hand has the button. A correct guess moves her up one step. A wrong guess keeps her where she is.

The button person keeps giving the seated children turns in order, until one reaches the top step. She then becomes the button person.

Be sure to discuss the *B* sound in these words: ball, basket, beanbag, balloon, button, bubbles.

Ideas to Reinforce the Letters *A* and *B*
Biscuits with Apple Butter

See recipe for Drop Biscuits on a packaged biscuit mix box. Children can stir the ingredients and spoon biscuits onto a baking sheet. When biscuits are done, cut them in half and spread them with butter and/or apple butter.

Apple and Banana Bobs

Skewer apple and banana slices with toothpicks. Other pieces of fruit (pineapple chunks, grapes, orange sections, maraschino cherries, and melon pieces) can also be used. If children are capable, they may skewer their own fruit.

While eating, talk about the different kinds of fruit God made and how Adam ate fruit from the trees in the garden God made for him. There was one tree God told him not to eat from, however; eventually, Adam disobeyed God and ate from that tree. Then God said he could not live in the garden any longer. (Genesis 3)

Discuss the words "apple" and "banana" which begin with the sounds children are learning. Include names of any children which begin with *A* or *B*.

Make sure the children's hands are clean. Give them some alphabet-shaped cereal. Let them look for the *A* and *B* shapes.

Point out the letters *A* and *B* on the front of the cereal box. Then show the children how to put cereal pieces in a straight line to make a number one. Also form capitals *A* and *B* with cereal before eating.

Fold on lines to make a mini book about Adam.

One man and one woman.

It was one sin too much.

One tree not to touch!

One day they gave in.

Shining Star Publications, Copyright © 1993

13

SS2827

Chapter 2

C is for Clothes. *D* is for Dorcas.

Dorcas
Tune: "London Bridge"

(Children hold hands and walk in a circle while singing all but the last line of each verse. On the last line, children raise their arms, still holding hands, and walk to the center of the circle. Then they back out and repeat the steps on each verse.)

Dorcas working for the Lord, for the Lord, for the Lord.
Dorcas working for the Lord…
Sew-ing dresses.

Dorcas working for the Lord, for the Lord, for the Lord.
Dorcas working for the Lord…
Mak-ing cookies.

Dorcas working for the Lord, for the Lord, for the Lord.
Dorcas working for the Lord…
Clean-ing houses.

Writing Skills

Repeat this rhyme while tracing the letter *C* on the alphabet page with your finger:
See the letter *C*.
(Teacher makes the sound of the letter *C* as in the word *cake*.) is its sound.
Start at the top … then come around.

Instruct the children to curve their left hands into a letter *C*. (If the teacher faces the children, she should use her right hand.)

Then show how to curve the right hand and place it against the open left hand to form a capital *D*.

Coordination Skill

Have jackets and shoes available for children to practice buttoning and zippering skills. Older children can practice tying shoe laces. You may want to have children who already know the skills teach those who do not.

D is for Dorcas.

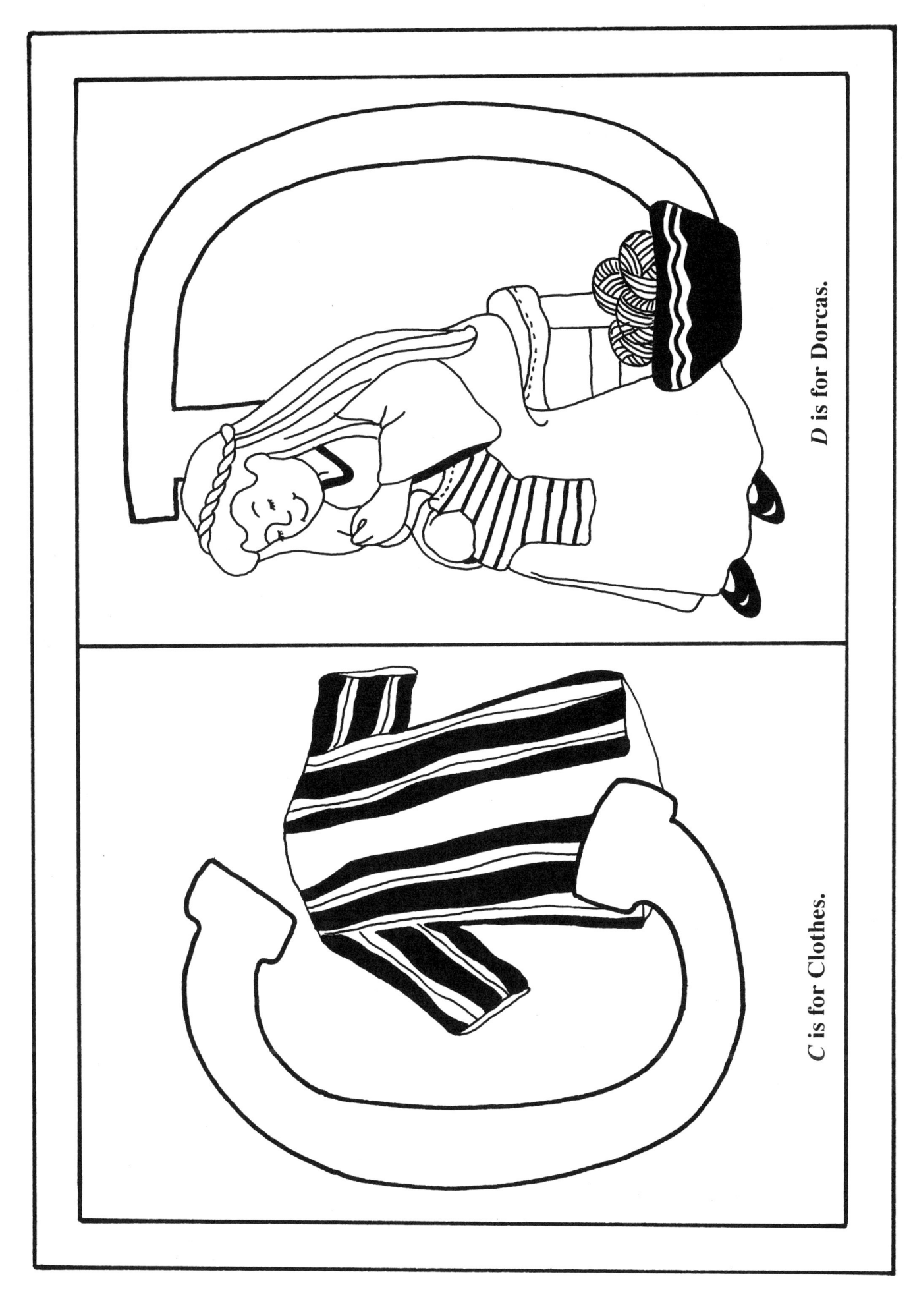

Color the frame purple.

C is for Clothes.

Color Fun: Purple People-Eater Puppet

The teacher puts a purple sock over her hand, forming a large "mouth" at the toe of the sock. Tell the children it is a Purple People-Eater Puppet.

Explain how the Purple People-Eater likes to say a word and have children guess the beginning sound of the word. When a child guesses incorrectly, he "eats her" (takes a small bite of her–makes it more like a tickle). When a child guesses correctly, he picks up a purple jelly bean with his "mouth" and drops it into the child's hand. If you don't want to use candy, use purple stickers or squares cut from purple construction paper.

Include the words *Adam, apple, animal, Bible, button, balloon, ball, bubbles, clothes, cloth, color, Dorcas, deeds, do,* and *did*. Also include food ideas from the lessons and children's names which begin with the letters *A, B, C,* and *D*.

For a treat, serve purple punch or grape juice and frozen grape juice bars.

Number Fun: Two

Ask the children "Do we have two heads? Two eyes? Two ears? Two noses? Two mouths? Two arms? Two thumbs? Two hands? Two tummies?"

Then ask them to tell you which body parts we have two of. This will reinforce the exercise.

If you sew two eyes, two ears, and one tongue on the Purple People-Eater Puppet, you can ask the children how many eyes, ears, mouths, and tongues the puppet has.

Point to body parts as you do this exercise (remember to go slowly at first):

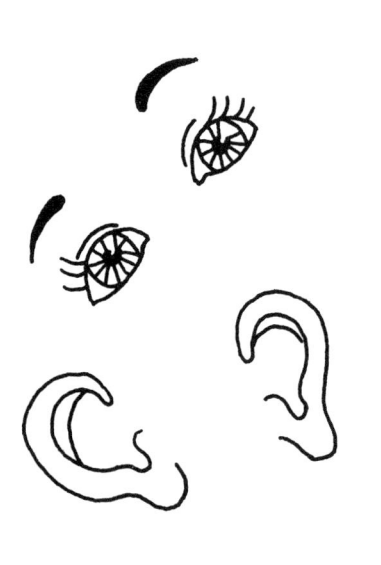

With two little eyes I see.

My ears are one and two.

I use two feet, two legs, two hands

When I have work to do.

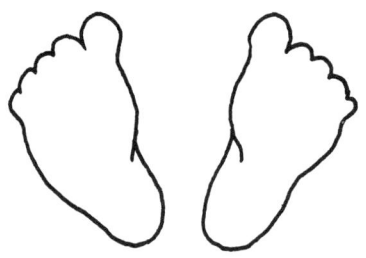

The Bible tells us Dorcas "was always doing good and helping the poor." It refers to "robes and other clothing" Dorcas had made for the people. (See Acts 9:36-42.)

The way Dorcas helped people was sewing for them. We may take some liberties with the passage, and assume she helped in other ways, too.

Helping Other People
Tune: "Mulberry Bush"

Do you see Dorcas, kind and good,
Kind and good, kind and good?
Do you see Dorcas, kind and good,
Helping other people?

This is the way she sews the clothes,
Sews the clothes, sews the clothes.
This is the way she sews the clothes,
Helping other people.

(Pretend to pull a needle in and out an imaginary cloth.)

This is the way she makes a cake,
Makes a cake, makes a cake.
This is the way she makes a cake,
Helping other people.

(Pretend to hold a bowl in one arm, stirring with the other.)

We can be like her, kind and good,
Kind and good, kind and good.
We can be like her, kind and good,
Helping other people.

This is the way we scrub a tub,
Scrub a tub, scrub a tub.
This is the way we scrub a tub,
Helping other people.

(Make scrubbing motion.)

This is the way we clean our jeans,
Clean our jeans, clean our jeans.
This is the way we clean our jeans,
Helping other people.

(Pretend to rub something up and down in a tub.)

Coach children to think of other ways they can be good helpers, and sing about them, too. (For example, pick up toys, make our bed, sweep the floor, set the table.)

Phonics Skill

Dorcas, Dorcas, did kind deeds,
Daily helping others' needs.
What does your friend do for you?
What kind deeds can you do, too?
(Emphasize words that begin with *D*. Discuss kind things friends do for each other.)

Tune: "Row, Row, Row Your Boat"

Close, close, close the door.	*(Clap on italicized words.)*
I'm putting on my clothes.	*(Pretend to dress.)*
Closer, closer, closer, closer–	*(Extend arms out from sides. Move hands closer together on each word, but don't let them meet.)*
Now the door is *closed*.	*(Clap on italicized word.)*

(Emphasize *C* words, but also discuss how the words *close, clothes, closer, closed* sound alike but mean different things.)

Craft Idea: Paper Vests, a Dorcas Project

Dorcas made clothes for other people. Your children will enjoy decorating vests for each other. Have them choose a partner. Be sure they understand they won't keep the vests they decorate–they will be for their partners, and the partners will decorate vests for them. This will help them understand the "Dorcas principle."

Materials:
a vest cut out of a grocery sack (Be careful not to cut away the glued parts.)
markers or poster paints
stickers, buttons, rickrack, lace, sequins for decorations

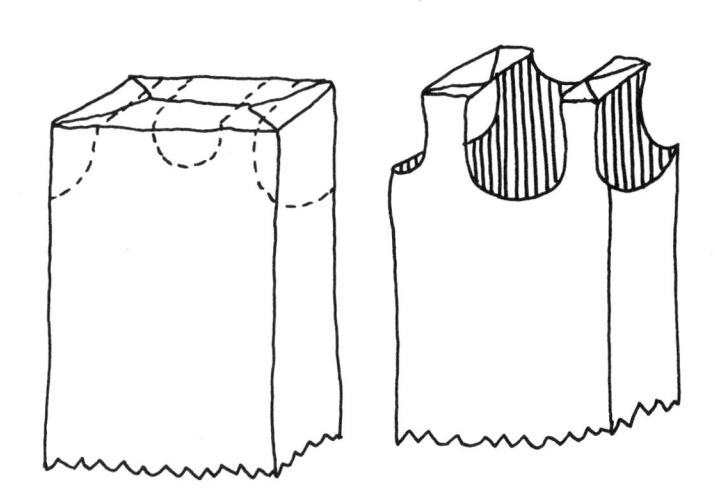

Shining Star Publications, Copyright © 1993   SS2827

Let's Pretend: Ways to Help

With younger children, let them guess what you are doing. Say "I'm a good helper. What am I doing?"

Suggested actions:
sweeping the floor
raking the lawn
picking flowers (smell them, admire them)
picking apples (polish one and eat it)
stirring soup (blow it cool and taste it)
dusting the furniture

After the children guess what you are doing, they can pretend to do it, too.

With older children, let them do the suggested actions. Some will even think up their own ideas. If you cannot guess what they are doing, asking for clues is better than giving up.

Variation:
Tell the children they will pretend to eat a meal using their best manners.

Teacher:

Our hands are dirty. What should we do?	*(Pretend to wash hands.)*
It's time to eat. Let's all sit nicely at the table.	*(Do so.)*
What do we do before we eat?	*(Thank God for the food–bow quietly and pray.)*
What do we do with our napkins?	*(Pretend to open and lay them in our laps.)*
Now let's pass the food and put some on our plates.	*(Do so. Pretend to eat.)*
What do we do with the arms we're not eating with?	*(We put them in our laps.)*
We have food on our chins. What should we do?	*(Wipe it with pretend napkins.)*
Now we are finished eating. What should we do with our dishes?	*(Take them to the sink.)*
Uh oh! There are crumbs on the floor. What should we do?	*(Pretend to sweep them.)*

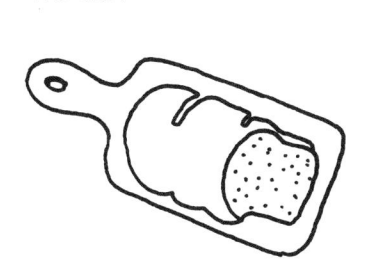

Counted Cross-Stitch Picture to Color

Use a purple crayon or a marker to color only the squares marked by +.

Ideas to Reinforce the Letters *C* and *D*

Choose any of the following:

carrot curls (peeled-off strips)

coconut cookies (macaroons)

cucumber "coins" (slices)

crackers

candy

caramel corn

cone cupcakes (Put 1/4 c. cake batter in each flat-bottom cone. Set cones in a muffin pan. Bake 15-18 minutes.)

dough (bread/cookie)

diced dates

drinks

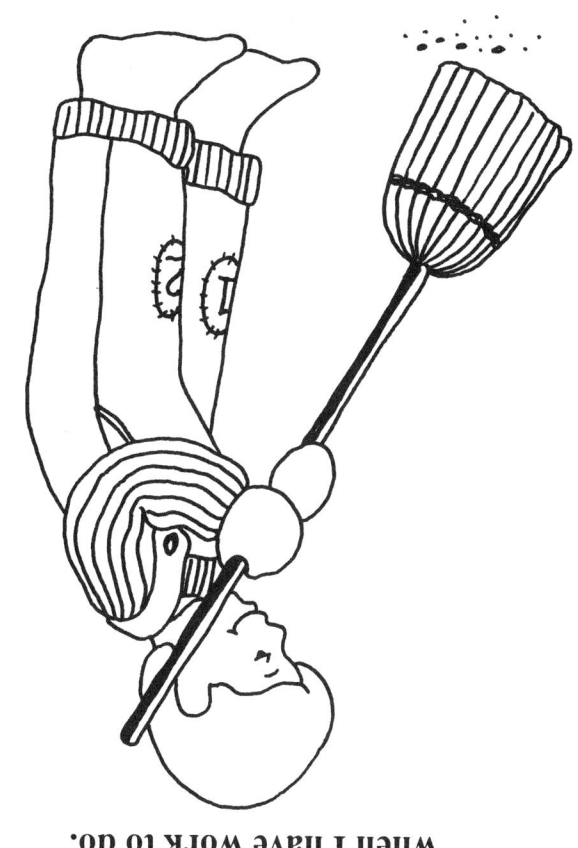

Fold on lines to make a mini book about the number two.

when I have work to do.

With two little eyes I see.

My ears are one and two.

I use two feet, two legs, two hands

Chapter 3

E is for Elijah. *F* is for Food.

Elijah
Tune: "The Farmer in the Dell"

Elijah by the brook.	(I Kings 17:1-7)
Elijah by the brook.	
Overhead a bird drops bread…	*(Children hold hands and walk in a*
Elijah by the brook.	*line around the room.)*
Elijah in the town.	(I Kings 17:8-16)
Elijah in the town.	
Eating cakes a woman makes…	*(Children form a circle, still holding*
Elijah in the town.	*hands.)*
Elijah by the tree.	(I Kings 19:1-9)
Elijah by the tree.	
Eating things an angel brings…	*(Children crouch down, still in a*
Elijah by the tree.	*circle.)*

Number Fun: Three of Each

Lesson to discuss: God provided three places for Elijah to stay and three ways for Elijah to eat.

Elijah stays by a brook.	*(Hold up one finger.)*
Elijah stays in a town.	*(Hold up two fingers.)*
Elijah stays under a tree.	*(Hold up three fingers.)*
Elijah eats food from a raven.	*(Hold up one finger.)*
Elijah eats food from a woman.	*(Hold up two fingers.)*
Elijah eats food from an angel.	*(Hold up three fingers.)*

How many *E* words can the children hear in the last three sentences?

How many words begin with the sound of the letter *F* as in the word *fun*?

Challenge children to find three small things, point to three large things, name three orange things, hold up three fingers, clap three times, etc. Count 1-2-3 for each exercise.

F is for Food.

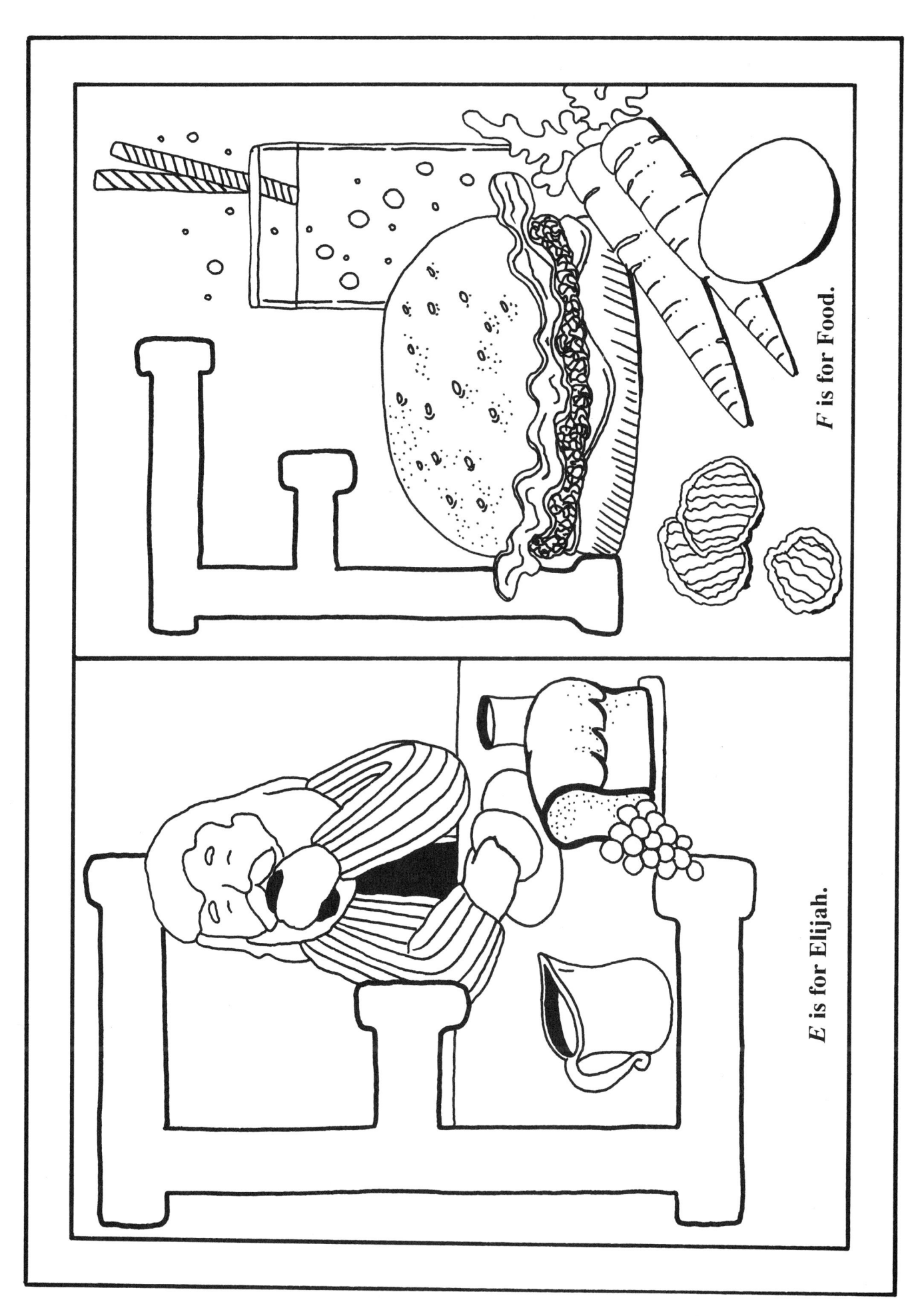

E is for Elijah.

Color the frame orange.

Color Fun: Orange

Note to teacher:
This page is for instructional coloring. Encourage the children to follow your directions for this color-review exercise, but remember the process is more important than the product.

Begin by discussing what foods are pictured and whether or not the children like to taste and smell those foods.

At first, the only color a child should have is an orange marker or crayon. Discuss which foods to color orange, and make sure the children see the letter *E* on those foods. Then have them color only the foods marked with *E*.

Do the same with the purple color and the letter *F*.

To review the blue color, they may try to color the dishes and fork blue.

Praise all efforts. The important thing is not neatness, but recognizing and using the correct color.

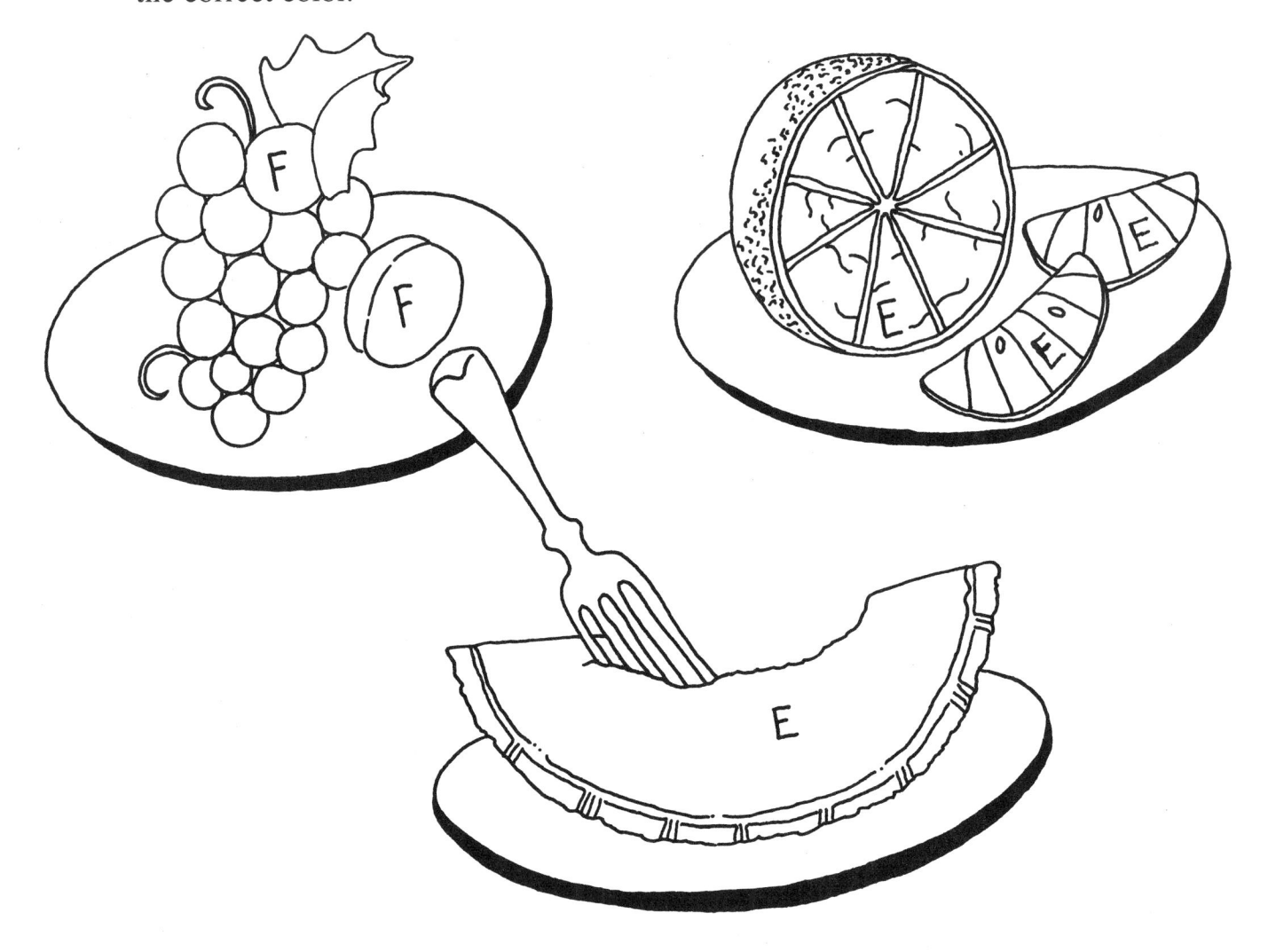

Phonics Skill

The letter *E* has two main sounds, long and short. So far, the children have identified the long sounds in the words *Elijah* and *eats*. Help them learn the difference between the long and short sounds in this sentence:

Ethan **E**vans **e**ats **e**ggs **e**very **e**vening.

Ask them to hold up their fingers every time they hear the sound of the letter *F* as in the word *fish*.

Four **f**unny **f**ish **f**lipped their **f**ins and **f**loated **off**.

(Emphasize the letters in bold type.)

Auditory Skill: Egg Shakers

At a craft store, buy plastic eggs that come apart in the middle, or save egg containers from panty hose. If these cannot be obtained, matchboxes that slide open will do. Let the children see what goes into the eggs. Shake each one after it is closed to see what sound it makes. Put the following items in the containers:

one penny . . . in two of them
two macaroni noodles . . . in two of them
three grains of rice . . . in two of them

Then mix them up and have children take turns finding sounds that match. When they think they have a match, open the eggs to see if they are correct.

Repeat the game using the following:
one button
two safety pins
three cotton balls

The following poem can be used with this exercise:

The eggs are not empty—each egg has a sound.
To hear with your ear, just shake it around.

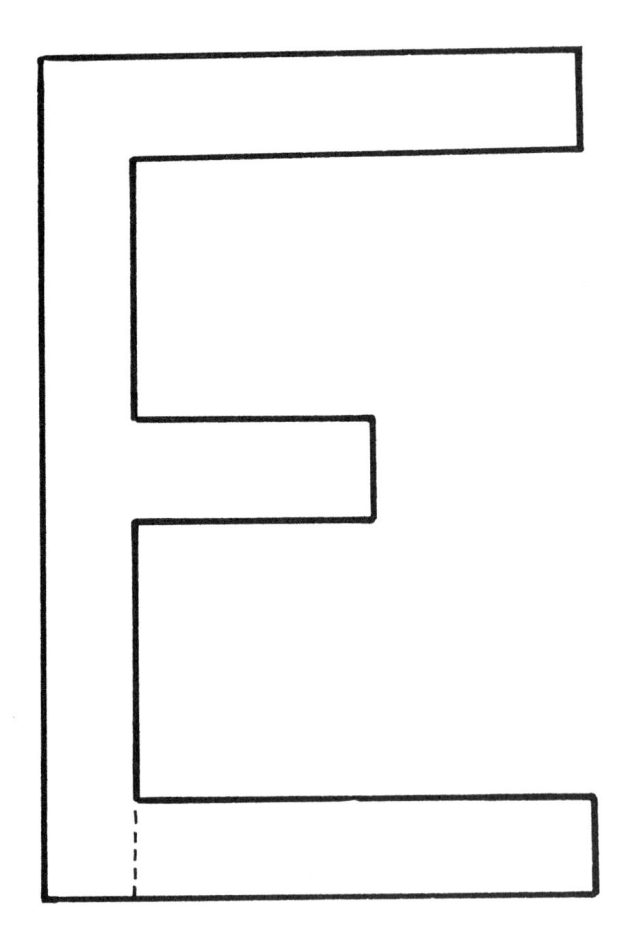

Note to teacher:
Cut out the letter *E*. Show it to the children and have them say its name.

Then fold the bottom strip back to make an *F*, and have them say its name.

Do this several times until the children can make the distinction.

Craft: Making *E*'s and *F*'s

Cut plastic straws into three-inch and one-inch lengths. Give each child one long piece and three short ones. Practice counting the short ones.

Show children how to form a letter *E* with the straw pieces. Show them which pieces to take away to form the letter *F*.

Optional: Help them glue straw letters to colored paper, making *E* on one half and *F* on the other half like the alphabet page. (See p. 23.)

Note to teacher:
Toothpicks which will not roll away may be substituted for the straw pieces.

Ask four children to lie on the floor in the shape of a letter *E*. Let the children tell you which child should get up to make an *F*. (The children would love it if the teacher would lie down to be the long vertical part of the letters.)

Making F's and E's
Tune: "Merrily, We Roll Along"

Merrily, we make an *F*, make an *F*, make an *F*.   *(Write on the board.)*
Merrily, we make an *F*. *F* is sure to please.

Add a line, and we will find, we will find, we will find.
Add a line, and we will find all the *F*'s are *E*'s.

Let's Pretend: Feeding Elijah

Elijah was a man of God called a prophet. He lived many years ago when the land of Israel was ruled by kings and queens.

One time there was no rain on the land for three and a half years. (James 5:17) What happened to the rivers and lakes? What happened to the fruit trees? What happened to the gardens without any rain to make them grow?

People were running out of food, but God took care of the people who loved God. Here's how God took care of Elijah.

First, God told Elijah to live beside a brook. Let's pretend we are drinking water from a brook. (Do so.) God made some birds called ravens fly to Elijah every morning and every evening. Let's be ravens and fly around the room. (Flap arms and move around the room while continuing to talk.) God caused the ravens to carry bread and meat in their beaks. When they got to where Elijah was, they dropped it to him. Elijah had plenty to eat and drink, until…(Stop flying.)

With no rain on the land, what happened to the brook? Yes, it dried up, and Elijah had nothing to drink. God told him to go to a town, and a woman would give him food.

Elijah obeyed and found a woman out gathering sticks to build a fire. (Let's gather sticks, too.) Elijah said to her, "Please bring me some water and bread." The woman didn't have much, but she put some oil and flour in a bowl and stirred it around (pretend to do so) until it all stuck together. Then she patted it with her hands (do so) and baked it. Elijah stayed in the town many days, and the woman always had enough cakes to feed Elijah and her family, too.

After this, God told Elijah to move again. This time he slept under a tree. There was no food there in the wilderness, but God took care of Elijah again. He sent an angel to feed him. Let's be angels coming down from heaven. (Hold arms out from sides and glide around the room while talking.) The angel fed Elijah baked bread and water. The Bible says that, strengthened by that food, Elijah was able to travel forty days and forty nights.

Note to teacher:
Now would be a good time to review the song on page 22.

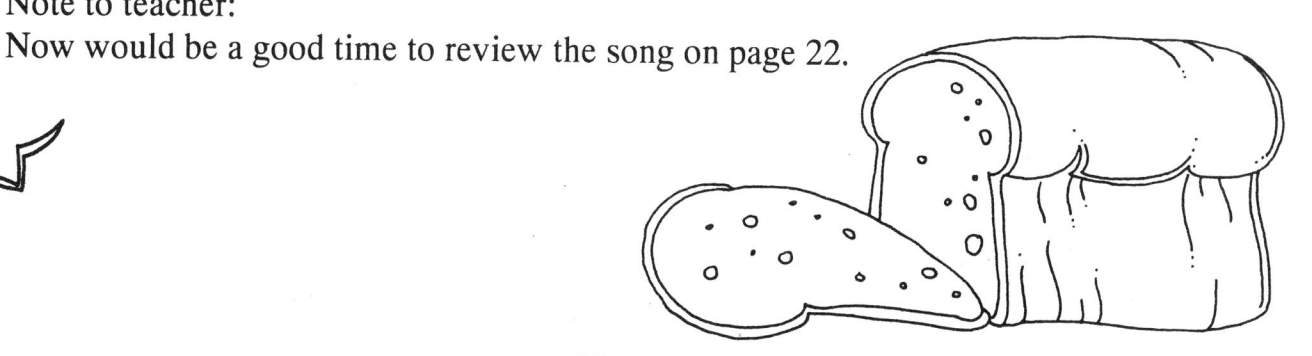

Review Game: Letter Spin

Divide a paper plate into six sections. Write one letter, *A* through *F*, in each section.

Cut a spinner out of poster board and attach it to the center of the plate with a metal brad.

Make one for each two to three children. They can take turns spinning and saying the letter indicated by the arrow.

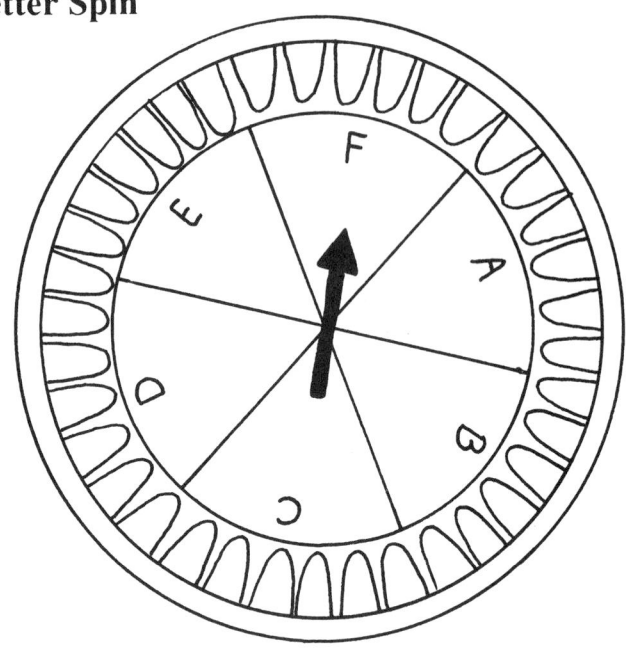

Recipe: Edible Play Dough

Mix one part of each of the following:
peanut butter
powdered sugar
corn syrup
powdered milk

Children can do the mixing. They might enjoy making a cake for Elijah like the woman did. Some children will want to eat it; others will save it. Let them know it's okay to eat this play dough but not the kind you buy in a store.

Ideas to Reinforce the Letters *E* and *F* and the Color Orange

Give each child a paper cup containing eight half-inch carrot slices. (Slice carrots to form small round pieces.) Use seven carrot slices to form the letter *F*. Add one carrot slice to change the letter *F* to letter *E*.

Following is a list of more foods which can be used to reinforce this lesson:
orange sections
orange juice
frozen orange juice bars

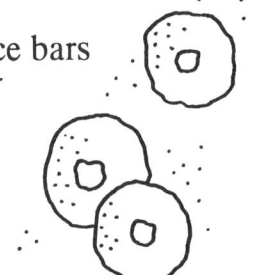

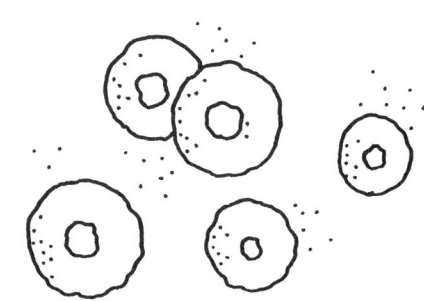

Fold on lines to make a mini book about Elijah.

Elijah eats food from a raven.

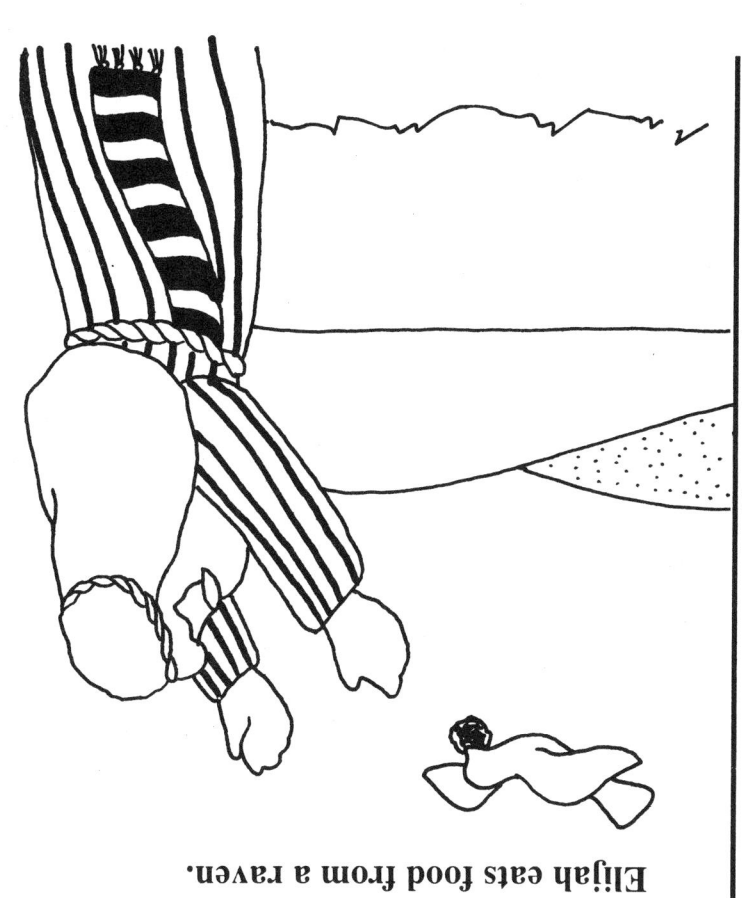

God takes care of Elijah.

Elijah eats food from a woman.

Elijah eats food from an angel.

Chapter 4

G is for Gift. *H* is for Hannah.

Hannah
Tune: "Are You Sleeping?"
Teacher sings one line at a time with children repeating.

Hannah, Hannah

Is so sad,

'Cause she wants a baby,

So she prays.

Hannah, Hannah

Is so glad.

Now she has a baby,

Sam-u-el, Sam-u-el.

Object Lesson: God's Good Gifts

Gift wrap a box and its lid separately, so the lid lifts off without unwrapping. Place a big bow on the lid. Inside the box have the following:
a small doll wrapped in a cloth
a picture of Jesus
a heart cut out of paper
a coat cut out of paper, or a small doll's coat
the letter *G* cut out of paper

Remove the items from the box one at a time and talk about the following:
doll–Samuel was a gift for Hannah. Every child is a gift from God to his parents.
Jesus–Jesus is God's gift to us.
heart–Jesus loves us so much He died for us and came back to life. This love is His gift to us.
coat–Hannah gave Samuel a gift every year–a coat.
G–G is for gift. (Teacher makes the sound of the letter *G* as in the word *gift*.)

H is for Hannah.

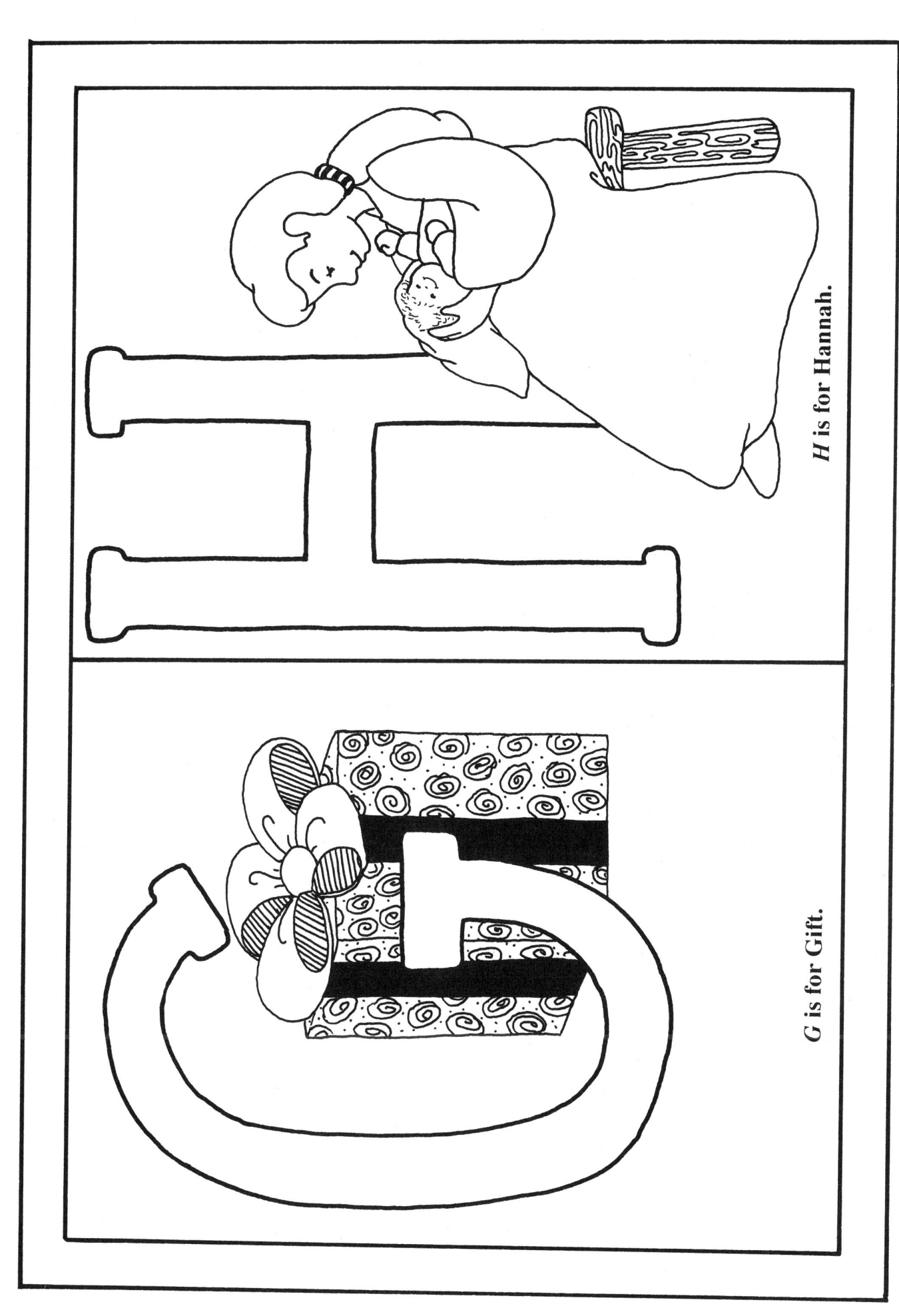

G is for Gift.

Color the frame green.

Number Fun: Four Sticks

Give each child four craft sticks or cotton swabs. The teacher will mark a pattern on the chalkboard and ask the children to use their sticks to copy the pattern.

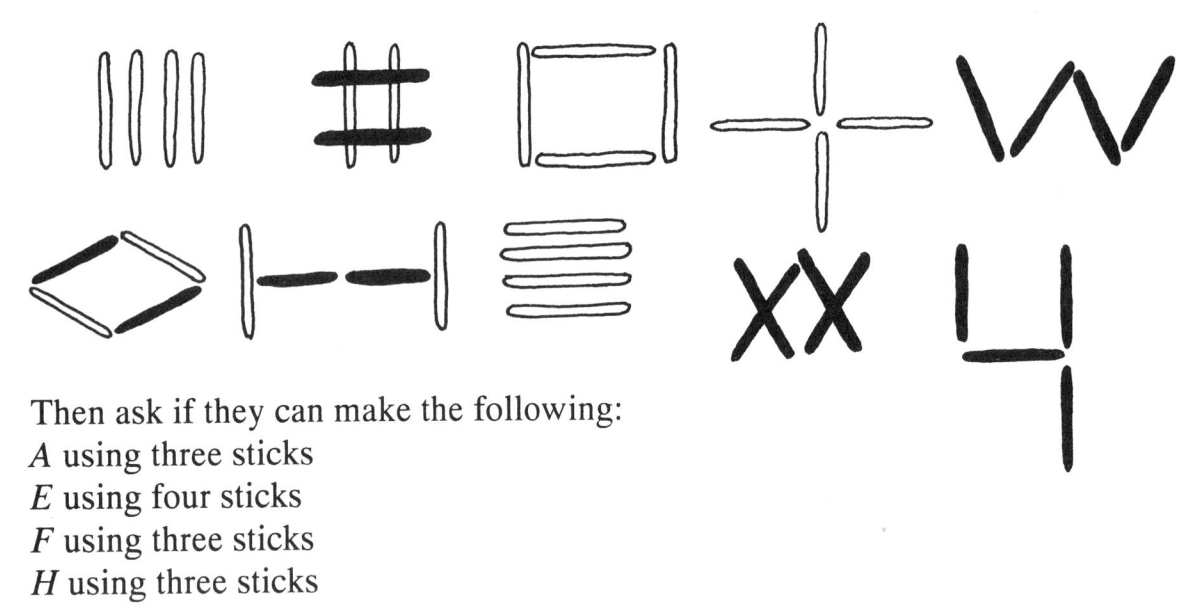

Then ask if they can make the following:
A using three sticks
E using four sticks
F using three sticks
H using three sticks

Whole-Body Activity

Use this activity when children need to line up at the door:
1-2-3-4 We are <u>hopping</u> to the door.
1-2-3-4 We are waiting by the door.

Substitute these words where underlined:
marching, walking, skipping

Color Fun: Green Hide-and-Seek

Use four green lids from gallon jugs of punch or milk. Have children cover their eyes while someone hides the lids around the room. Then children search until all the lids are found. Count them each time. Take turns hiding them until everyone has had a turn. Ask children to point out other things that are green.

For a treat, serve green grapes or frozen juice bars, and green punch.

What Hannah Made
Tune: "The Muffin Man"

Oh, do you know what Hannah made? *(Make sewing motions.)*
  What Hannah made? What Hannah made?
Oh, do you know what Hannah made?
  She made a little coat.

Oh, do you know what Samuel wore? *(Wrap arms around self.)*
  What Samuel wore? What Samuel wore?
Oh, do you know what Samuel wore?
  He wore the little coat.

Let's Pretend
Tune: "She'll Be Comin' 'Round the Mountain"

Explain how young Samuel went to live in the tabernacle. It was like a large church building, but the people who took care of it lived there. Samuel helped with the work as much as he was able. Name things a young child could do; then pretend to do them, using this song.

Samuel is a happy helper for the Lord.	*(Clap hands twice.)*
Samuel is a happy helper for the Lord.	*(Clap hands twice.)*
Samuel is a happy helper. Samuel is a happy helper.	
Samuel is a happy helper for the Lord.	*(Clap hands twice.)*

Here's how Samuel <u>sweeps the corners</u> for the Lord.	*(Make sweeping motions.)*

(Continue as above.)
Substitute these words for the underlined words:

lights the candles	*(Touch index finger to fingertips on the other hand.)*
wipes the tables	*(Make wiping motions.)*
folds his laundry	*(Make folding motions.)*
shakes the blankets	*(Make shaking motions.)*
empties garbage	*(Make dumping motions.)*

Here's how I can sweep and vacuum for the Lord. *(Make pushing motions.)*
(Continue with substituted words as above.)

I can be a happy helper for the Lord. *(Clap hands twice.)*
(Continue as in first verse.)

(Children may think of other things they can do to be helpful.)

Phonics Skill

Ask children to identify the four words in each sentence that begin with the letter *G*.

Give a **g**ift of **g**orp to **G**randma.
God is **g**reat, and **G**od is **g**ood.

Ask children to identify the four words in each sentence that begin with the letter *H*.

Hannah **h**as **h**er **h**andsome son.
Happy **h**earts make **h**elpful **h**ands.

Craft: Sewing Cards
(develops eye-hand coordination)

Cut coat patterns out of card stock paper. (Old greeting cards will do.)
Punch holes around the edges.
Tape one end of a length of green yarn to make a needle, and tie a big knot in the other end.
Thread the yarn through one hole in the coat,
but let the children thread the other holes any way they desire.

Finger Play: Coat Buttons

1-2-3-4 buttons on my coat.	*(Poke chest four times.)*
1-2-3-4 buttonholes, too.	*(Repeat.)*
1-2-3-4 fingers and a thumb.	*(Hold up fingers one at a time, or point to fingers on the opposite hand.)*
Can they make the buttons go through?	*(Tickle self, or tickle child.)*

Give a Gift of Gorp

Cut rectangles of paper which will fit around 6-ounce juice cans you have collected for each child. Let the child decorate the paper. Wrap it around the can, and tape or glue it in place. (Optional: glue ribbons as trim around the top and bottom of the can.)

Give each child a sandwich bag to fill with gorp. Gorp is any combination of the following:

sunflower seeds	raisins	dry cereal
dried fruit pieces	nuts	coconut

This can be premixed, or children can spoon the ingredients from separate bowls.

Help each child put the bag into the can she decorated, and tape the bag shut. A ribbon bow can go around the top of the bag.

The child can give this craft as a gift. When the gorp is gone, the can becomes a pencil holder.

Review Exercise: Half-Heart Puzzles

Cut four hearts out of green construction paper. Then cut the hearts in half so the sides fit together like a puzzle.

Put one, two, three, or four dots on one half of the heart puzzle; number 1, 2, 3, or 4 on the other half to correspond to the dots. Children can match the number to the amount of dots.

For alphabet review, cut out eight more hearts, and then cut each heart in half so it fits together like a puzzle. Put matching capital letters on both sides of each heart. (Use letters *A* through *H*, one letter for each of the eight hearts.) Children try to recognize which letters are alike, and if the puzzle fits, they are correct.

Ideas to Reinforce the Letters *G* and *H* and the Color Green

green grapes	gum drops	heart-shaped cookies

Use the grapes or gum drops to form the letters *G* and *H* before eating.

Fold on lines to make a mini book about counting to four.

1-2-3-4 buttons on my coat.

Can they make the buttons go through?

1-2-3-4 buttonholes, too.

1-2-3-4 fingers and a thumb.

Chapter 5

I is for Israel.   *J* is for Joshua.

Crossing the Jordan
Tune: "Dem Bones, Dem Bones, Dem Dry Bones"

Joshua 3 tells us the story of Israel crossing the Jordan River. Joshua was the leader of the people of Israel at that time. This song acquaints young children with two *J* words and one *I* word (Jordan, Joshua, Israel), and the concept of five.

For the song, choose five children to hold on to each other at the waist and march around the room while everyone sings. On the last line of each verse, say the name of the person at the front, and he sits down.
*Children wiggle their hips on the BOOMS.

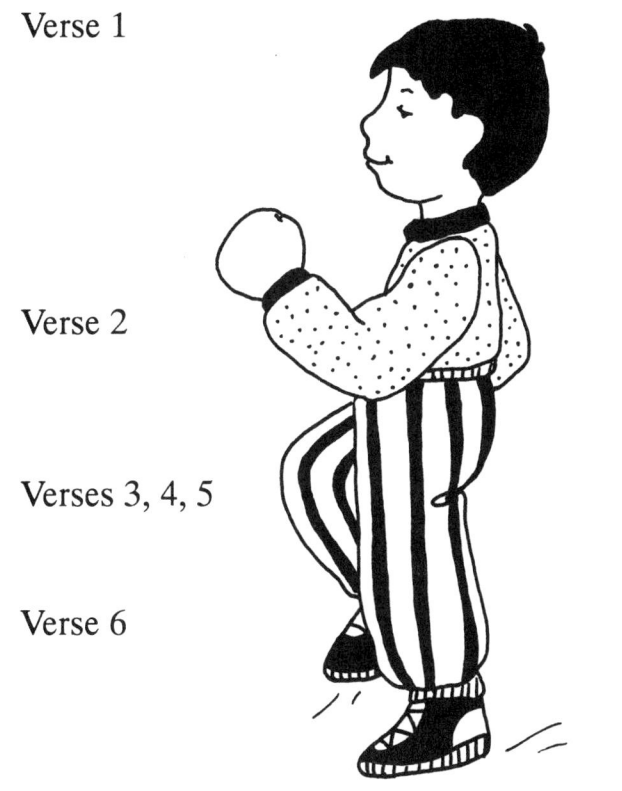

Verse 1

Crossing the Jordan, take five steps.
Crossing the Jordan, take five steps.
Crossing the Jordan, take five steps.
Now _____ is across.

Boom, Boom, Boom*

Verse 2

Crossing the Jordan, take four steps.

(Continue as above.)

Verses 3, 4, 5

(Continue with three steps, two steps, one step.)

Verse 6

Crossing the Jordan, take no steps.
Crossing the Jordan, take no steps.
Crossing the Jordan, take no steps.
Now ISRAEL is across.

Finger Play: This Is One
(Hold up the number of fingers indicated and do the action.)

This is one. *Touch your tongue.*
This is two. *Touch your shoe.*
This is three. *Touch your knee.*
This is four. *Touch the floor.*
This is five. *Come alive! (Move hands all around.)*

J is for Joshua.

I is for Israel.

Color the frame grey.

Color Fun: A Grey Picture

Have children hold up a grey crayon. Tell them to think about some things that are this color while they listen to this poem:

> Grey is smoke. Grey is cats,
> Grandma's hair, Grandpa's hat.
> Elephants and mice are grey
> And the gum I chew all day.

Instruct the children to color the grey things in this picture as you tell them the story. (Pause while they are coloring.)

A grey cat
chased a grey mouse
down a grey sidewalk
into a grey house.

Who's watching the grey cat
on a grey fence
under the grey smoke
of the grey house?

It's a grey-haired grandma
and the little grey mouse.

Number Fun: How Many?

How many fingers on my hand? 1-2-3-4-5.	*(Hold up one hand and point to fingers as you count.)*
Wiggle them; wave them; shake them alive:	*(With both hands, do what the words indicate.)*
1-2-3-4-5.	*(Hold up fingers one at a time.)*
How many toes on my foot? 1-2-3-4-5.	*(Point to toes on one foot.)*
Stomp them; march them; walk them alive:	*(With both feet, do what the words indicate.)*
1-2-3-4-5.	*(March to the beat as you count.)*

Letter-Recognition Games

Pinch Me
Mark a paper plate into ten sections. Put one letter, A through J, in each section. Name a letter, and let a child mark it with a pinch-type clothespin.

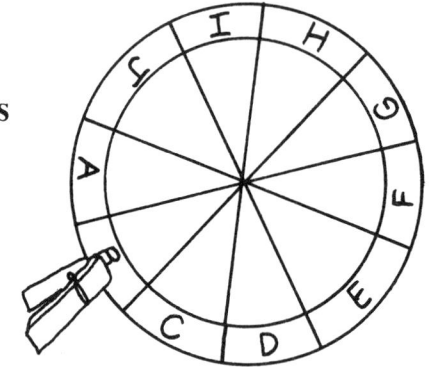

Match Me
Cut twenty uniform rectangles out of heavy paper or tagboard. Make two cards with *A*, two with *B*, and so on through *J*.

Turn the cards letter-side down and arrange them in two rows of ten, or four rows of five.

One child at a time turns over two cards, naming the letters on them. If they match, he keeps them and takes another turn. If they don't match, he turns them face-down again, in their places, and the next child takes a turn.

If adults and children are playing together, children get double turns.

Phonics Skill: Vowel Sound

Review the letters *A* and *E* to remind the children that some letters have more than one sound. The letter *I* is like this, too.

The letter *I* makes two sounds.
The short *I* is the first sound you hear in the word *Israel*.

The long *I* is the first sound you hear in the word *ice*.

Let's Pretend: The Fall of Jericho (Joshua 6:1-21)

Set chairs in the center of the room to represent Jericho. Have the chairs face each other so their backs are like a wall. The children will march around "Jericho." Use cardboard tubes for trumpets.

Jericho was a city. God told Joshua to destroy it, but Jericho had a strong wall around it. Joshua and his men could never get through it or tear it down, so God told Joshua what to do.

The people of Israel got up early one morning. Seven of them had trumpets, but all of you may have one. The people marched around Jericho's wall one time, blowing their trumpets. (Do so. This will probably work best if the teacher leads the children. The preschool child likes to imitate.) Then they went back to their camp.

The next day, Joshua and the people did the same thing. They marched around Jericho, blowing their trumpets. (Do so.)

On the third day, guess what God wanted the people to do again. That's right–they marched around Jericho again. (Do so.)

The fourth day, they did the same thing. (March around chairs again.)

Now it's the fifth day; let's march again. (Do so.)

On the sixth day, they again marched and blew trumpets. (Do so.)

On the seventh day, Joshua and the people marched around Jericho seven times. Let's count them. (Do so.)

One. Two. Three. Four. Five. Six. Seven. Then they blew on their horns one long blast. (Do so.) The people shouted. (Do so.) The walls of Jericho fell down flat. (If "Jericho" consists of folding chairs, fold them and lay them flat. If not, lay chairs over on their backs. Keep open spaces between chairs so children can pass through.)

That's how God destroyed Jericho for Joshua and the people of Israel.

Game: Joshua at Jericho

This game can be played like Musical Chairs, but for preschoolers, have one chair for each child. This way no one is eliminated. The teacher can either stop playing music or interrupt the rhyme to signal the children to find a seat.

Children march around a circle of chairs as they hear this rhyme. The children will improve their listening skills by doing what the words indicate.

Joshua at Jericho,
March around it, so, so, so.
Faster, faster, go, go, go.
Slower, slower, slow, slow, slow.
Time to stop now, w-h-o-a.

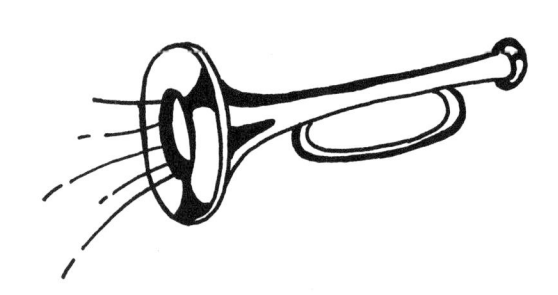

Game: Walk the Boxes

Place shoe boxes and gift boxes of different sizes on the floor, open side up. Form a path across the room. Children walk the path by placing one foot in a box for each step.
Note to teacher:
If boxes slip easily, put double-stick tape on the underneath side.

Game: Crossing Jordan

Place two yardsticks on the floor for the Jordan River. Explain how Israel crossed the river on dry ground because God held the water back. Pretend you are crossing the Jordan between the yardsticks, and do it like this:

Can you skip across? Can you hop across?
Can you jump across? Can you run across?
Can you walk backwards? Can you twirl?
Can you turn somersaults across?
Can you pretend to roll in a wheelchair?
Can you lie down and roll across?
Can you crawl across? Can you hold your breath?
Can you balance a book on your head?
Can you walk with your hands on your shoulders?

(Children might think of other things to do.)

Craft: Play-Dough Altars

After the Israelites crossed the Jordan River on dry ground, they thanked God by making a pile of twelve stones. This is called an altar to God. Show children how to roll play dough into balls and pile them up as "stones" on an altar. Any number of stones is all right.

Recipe for Grey Play Dough
- 4 cups boiling water
- 1/2 cup oil
- equal drops of red, blue, and yellow food color until liquid looks grey
- 1 cup salt
- 5 cups flour
- 2 tablespoons alum

Mix the first four ingredients. Add flour and alum. Knead with dough hooks, adding more flour and/or oil until dough is no longer sticky. If kneading by hand, use an oiled surface and wear rubber gloves until dough cools. To store, wrap in plastic wrap and keep in a closed container.

Ideas to Reinforce the Letters *I* and *J*

Ice Cube Gelatin

3 small boxes flavored gelatin
4 envelopes unflavored gelatin
4 cups boiling water

Mix until all is dissolved.
Pour into a 9" x 13" pan and refrigerate until firm.

Cut into cubes the size of ice cubes.
Eat as finger food.

Ice-Cold Juice

Mix a beverage from powdered concentrate, using half the water called for.

Put 3 cups at a time in a blender. Add 2 cups crushed ice. Blend until mixture is slushy. Serve with a spoon.

I J Sandwiches

To reinforce the letters *I* and *J*, make these open-faced sandwiches: Cut bread as illustrated to form *I*-shaped slices. Spread with jam for the letter *J*.

Fold on lines to make a mini book about the color grey.

Grey is smoke. Grey is cats,

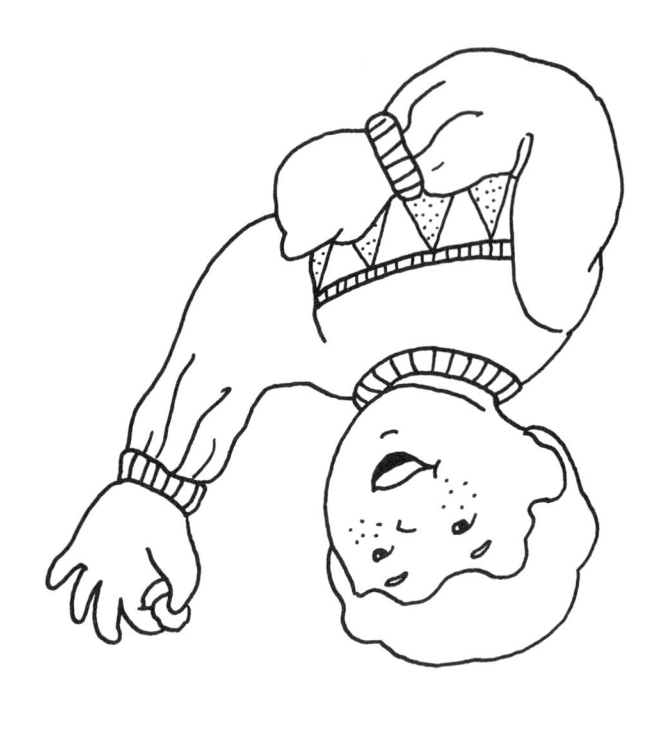

and the gum I chew all day.

Grandma's hair, Grandpa's hat.

Elephants and mice are grey

Chapter 6

K is for King. *L* is for Lamb.

David, the Shepherd
Tune: "Rise and Shine, and Give God the Glory, Glory"

Out in the pasture, he's watching the sheepy, sheepy.
Out in the pasture, he's watching the sheepy, sheepy.
Watch-ing o-ver all of the little sheepies,
David, shepherd boy.

Up in the palace, he's watching the people, people.
Up in the palace, he's watching the people, people.
Watch-ing o-ver all of the chosen people,
David, shepherd king.

Phonics Skill: Finger Play
Tune: "The Alphabet Song"

(Teacher makes the sound of the letter *L* four times.) Little lamb	*(Clap on the beat.)*
Ran and ran and ran and ran.	*(Run in place.)*
(Teacher makes the sound of the letter *K* four times.) David king	*(Clap on the beat.)*
Liked to sing and sing and sing.	*(Place hands on heart, one over the other; rock side-to-side.)*
I can run, and I can sing	*(Repeat running and singing motions.)*
Like the little lamb and king.	*(Clap on the beat.)*

L is for Lamb.

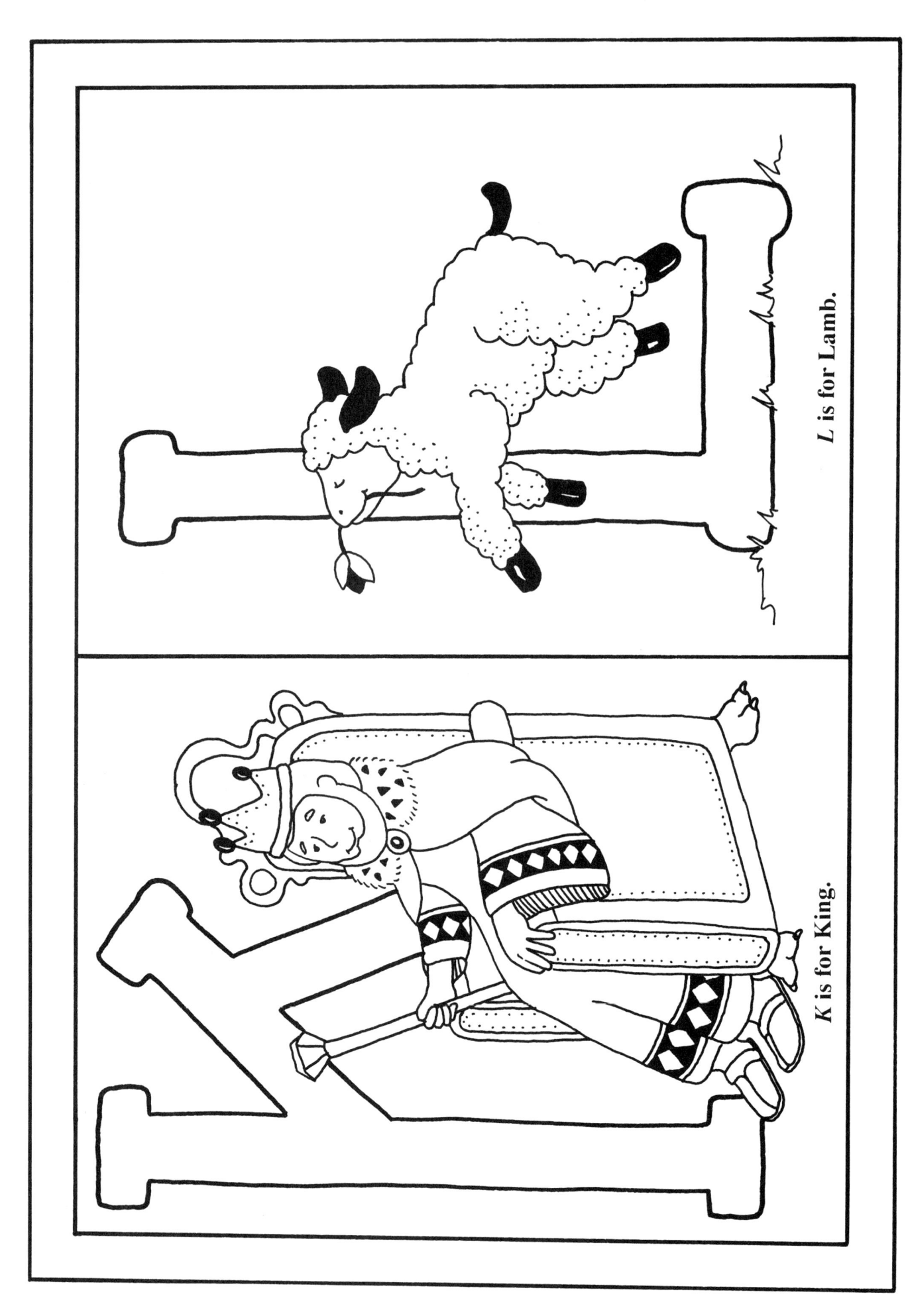

K is for King.

Color the frame brown.

Color Fun Craft: Little Brown Lambs

Cut out a lamb face for each child. Help him glue it to a brown paper bag. Ask children to pick a crayon or marker which is the same color as the brown bag. Color the lamb face brown.

Have each child put the lamb puppet over his hand and do this finger play.

Little brown lambs	*(Make puppet hand "walk" up other arm.)*
A-walking up the hill	
Stop to drink and	*(Make puppet hand "eat" out of other hand, palm open).*
Eat a meal.	
They run to the east.	*(Stretch puppet arm out to the right.)*
They run to the west.	*(Stretch puppet arm out to the left.)*
They all lie down	*(Place puppet hand in crook of other arm.)*
And take a rest.	

For a treat, serve brownies and chocolate milk or root beer.

Number Fun: Six Lambs

Give each child six cotton balls. Count them aloud as you pass them out. Have children keep them in a pile, picking them up one at a time on the bold words of this rhyme and placing them in another pile.

One lamb, **two** lambs, **three** lambs, **four**–
Look around and find some more.
More lambs–**five** lambs, **six** lambs now.
Count to six 'cause you know how.
(Count the cotton balls again).

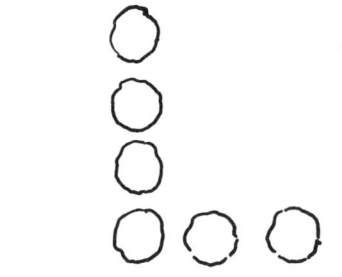

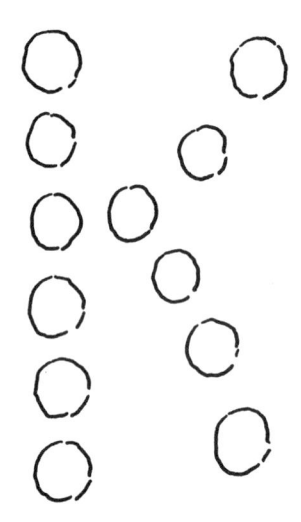

Draw circles on the board to show children how to place their cotton balls in two lines to make the letter *L*.

If children are capable, pass out six more cotton balls to form the letter *K*.

Game with Dice

Roll one die and count the dots. Do this several times until children become familiar with the procedure.

Note to teacher:
Unless you have exceptional preschoolers, they will not relate a number to dots without counting them.

Next roll six dice and put aside all those showing one dot. Have children continue rolling the remaining dice until all have shown one dot. Continue with two, etc. Count the dots on each die you save from a roll.

To introduce the concept of more/less have six children each roll one die at the same time. Ask whose die has the most dots. Count them. The teacher says "Six is more than three; two is more than one," etc.

If children respond well to this, do the same with the concept of whose die has the least. Say "Two is less than six; two is less than three," etc.

Auditory Skill: Musical Instruments

Children love to hear themselves make noise. God enjoys it, too. (Psalm 33:1-3; Psalm 98:4-6; Psalm 100:1-2) Help children learn that David wrote songs of praise to God and sang them to his sheep to calm them. David played a stringed instrument, too. Here are some instruments the children can "play."

Drum	A small plastic (stainless steel if you're brave) bowl turned upside down. Hit with a wooden spoon.
Shakers	Plastic spice bottles or 35 mm film cases filled with rice or small macaroni. Make sure lids are tight.
Strings	Thin rubber bands stretched around a small, strong box with a round hole cut in the lid.
Horn	Cardboard tube from roll of paper towels. Draw dots on the side. Hum through it.
Rattle	Ring of keys or metal measuring spoons on a ring.
Tambourine	Jingle bells threaded on a loop of yarn, or attached to an aluminum pie plate.
Cymbals	Two aluminum pie pans. Hold at the edge and hit backs together.
Rhythm Sticks	Two wooden spoons or dowel rods clapped together.

Sing together as the children play instruments. Because preschool children concentrate on one thing at a time, the teacher may be the only one singing. Exchange instruments often so everyone has a chance to try several or all of the instruments.

Suggested songs: simple praise songs with repetitive words

Tape recorder fun: Record the children singing and answering discussion questions. Play the recording back and let them identify who is speaking. They may not recognize their own voices.

Note to teacher:
If you give a program with a small number of children, record the children singing ahead of time. At the program, play the recording along with live singing to add volume and confidence.

Game: Sheepfold

Divide children into two teams. One team forms a sheepfold by holding hands in a circle. The other team inside the circle tries to get out of the fold by ducking under hands. Children holding hands try to prevent this by lowering their hands. (Remind them not to let go.) When all the "sheep" are out of the fold, they become the fold, and the other team gets a turn to be sheep.

A variation is to let children try to go through the opponent's hands. In this case, children form the circle by holding each other's wrists. Caution: Don't try this variation if your group includes a wide range of ages or sizes.

Game: Lost Sheep

Blindfold a child who is chosen to be the shepherd. Tell him all his sheep are lost, and he must find them.

Give sheep an opportunity to place themselves; then instruct them not to move. When everyone is ready, the shepherd calls "Sheep." All the sheep respond by saying "Baaaah" every time the shepherd says "Sheep." The shepherd must locate his sheep by listening.

When he touches a sheep, that sheep must go to a designated place (the fold) until all sheep have been found. The last sheep found becomes the new shepherd.

Craft: Cotton Sheep

Each child needs the following:
one sheet of blue construction paper
one-half sheet of green construction paper (torn in half lengthwise so it has a rough edge)
six cotton balls
brown marker or crayon
glue

Glue the green one-half sheet to the bottom of the blue paper so the corners match. Let each child glue his six cotton balls randomly on the green pasture. Show him how to draw four straight legs under each ball for legs. Count the legs as they are drawn. Count the sheep when the craft is complete.

Let's Pretend: Choosing a King

Choose children to be the following:

Samuel (Give him a little jar.)

Jesse and seven children to be the sons of Jesse (Put them in one area of the room.)

David (Put him in a corner to take care of sheep.)

Note to teacher:
If you do not have enough children, use dolls or puppets.

One day God told Samuel there would be a new king of Israel. He would be the son of a man named Jesse. Samuel went to Jesse's house. (Samuel goes to Jesse and his sons.)

He looked at Jesse's first son, and God said, "No." (Have each child stand before Samuel in turn, and Samuel shakes his head "No.") He looked at the second son. Again God said, "No." The third son came forward, and God said, "No." The fourth son came forward, and God said, "Not this one either." (Repeat for fifth son and sixth son.) Finally, the seventh son came forward, and again God said, "No".

Then Samuel asked, "Is this all the sons you have?"

Jesse answered, "I have one more, but he's the youngest. He's taking care of the sheep."

Samuel said, "Bring him here, for we will not sit down until he comes."

Someone went to get David. (Send one of the sons to do this.) When David came to Samuel, God said, "Anoint him, for this is the one."

Samuel took the oil and poured it on David's head. (Samuel pretends to do so.) This was a sign that David would be the next king of Israel. (All cheer.)

Ideas to Reinforce the Letters *K* and *L*

kiwifruit
chocolate kisses
licorice sticks
lemons
lime punch or lemonade

Show children a lime, lemon, and kiwifruit. Discuss how they are similar and how they are different. Let them taste the kiwifruit if they wish.

Fold on lines to make a mini book about counting to six.

Count to six 'cause you know how.

One lamb, two lambs, three lambs, four—

Look around and find some more.

More lambs—five lambs, six lambs now.

52

Chapter 7

M is for Mary.   *N* is for Night.

Jesus Was His Name
Tune: "Mary Had a Little Lamb"

Mary had a little Son,	*(Fold and rock arms across chest.)*
Little Son, little Son.	
Mary had a little Son, and Jesus was His name.	

Shepherds watching in the night,	*(Shade forehead with hand.)*
In the night, in the night.	
Shepherds watching in the night heard the angels sing.	

(Chorus)

Then they came to see God's Son,	*(Walk in place.)*
See God's Son, see God's Son.	
Then they came to see God's Son,	
And Jesus was His name.	

One night wise men saw a star,	*(Both hands form a telescope held*
Saw a star, saw a star.	*to one eye.)*
One night wise men saw a star in the eastern sky.	

Repeat chorus.

Number Fun: Counting to Seven
(Hold up fingers as you count.)

1-2-3-4-5-6-7. Jesus came to us from heaven.
7-6-5-4-3-2-1. Jesus is God's holy Son.

Mary had a little Son—God in flesh for everyone.
Jesus came from heaven above. How many people does He love?
1-2-3-4-5-6-7.

(Count to 7 as you point to children; repeat until everyone has been included.)

M is for Mary.

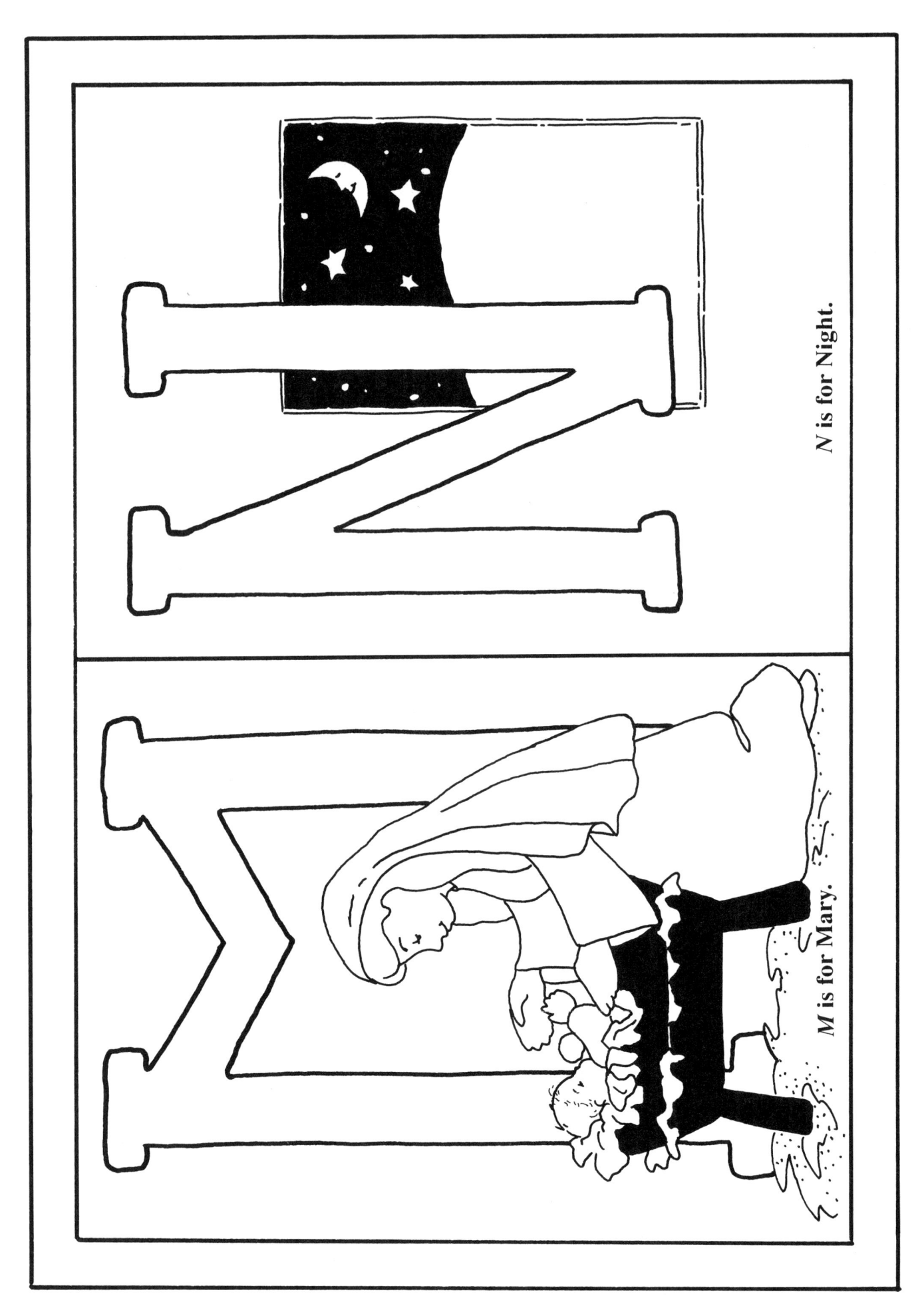

N is for Night.

Color the frame black.

Color Fun: Night Picture

On drawing paper, use a white crayon to make a moon and stars. Use a green crayon to make the horizon and trees. Press very hard so paint will not be absorbed.

Prepare one page for each student.

Dress children in paint shirts. Using either paint brushes or cotton swabs, let them paint over the page with black paint.

While they do this, discuss things we see in the sky at night. Ask these questions: What did the shepherds see in the sky when Jesus was born? (angels) What did wise men see in the sky when Jesus was born? (a new star) Practice the letter *N* sound for the word *night*. Talk about the color black.

Variations:
Use black construction paper and white chalk. Give paper and chalk to each child, and let the children draw a night picture. They are too young for controlled art, but ask them to draw a moon and stars. Praise whatever they draw. The effort is more important than the end result.

Most children this age love stickers. Let them put sticker stars on black construction paper for a night picture.

For a treat, serve black olives or black licorice.

Special Star
Tune: "Jingle Bells" chorus

Special star, special star   *(Hold one hand above head;*
  Shining in the night.   *open and close it.)*
Special star, special star
  In the East so bright.

Mary smiles, Mary smiles   *(Fold and rock arms as if*
  As the nighttime creeps.   *holding a baby.)*
Mary smiles, Mary smiles,
  And baby Jesus sleeps.

Phonics Skill

Emphasize sounds of the letters *M* and *N* as you say the following:

Mine, mine, mine, mine. Jesus is **mine.**
M-I-N-E. Jesus is **mine.**

Our Creator God
Tune: "We Wish You a Merry Christmas"

Do YOU know who made the **nighttime**?	*(Point to someone on each "You.")*
Do YOU know who made the **nighttime**?	
Do YOU know who made the **nighttime**?	
Our Cre-a-tor God.	*(Point up.)*

You may choose to substitute other words for nighttime: daytime, sunshine, blue sky, green grass, black cats, children, mothers, fathers, teachers, etc. Let children brainstorm more words. You may wish to distinguish between what God Himself created, and what He gives people the ability to make. If a child wants to sing about tables, for example, the last line could be "A person with skill."

Let's Pretend: Taking Care of Baby Jesus

Taking care of baby Jesus.	*(Cradle and rock arms.)*
Morning, noon, and night.	
Taking care of baby Jesus.	
Wrap Him up in white.	*(Roll hands over each other.)*
Taking care of baby Jesus.	
Mary's sweet delight.	*(Fold hands over heart.)*
Taking care of baby Jesus.	
Mary did it right.	*(Cradle and rock arms.)*

Alphabet Review

Make a copy for each child. Show the children how to connect the letters A through L in sequence to make a 7, M, and N.

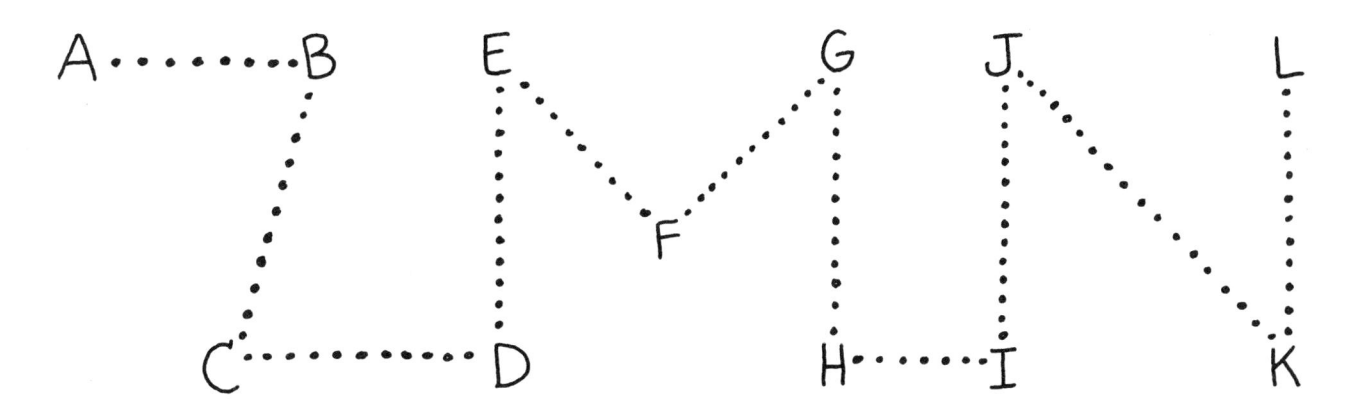

Alphabet and Number Review Game: Trim the Tree
(Children enjoy this game, even if it's not December.)

Materials:
one yard green felt (Cut out an evergreen tree from an enlarged pattern.)
blue felt (Cut out twelve ball ornaments.)
purple felt (Cut out twelve bells.)
orange felt (Cut out twelve angels.)
Adjust patterns at the bottom of the page to the desired size.

Use cards with a number (1-7) and the pages from an alphabet book. Let children "trim the Christmas tree" when they correctly identify a number 1-7, a letter A through N, or can give its sound.

If you have a classroom of children, divide them into three teams. Otherwise, let each child choose an ornament when he gets a right answer. (Ask him what color ornament he chose).

Note to teacher:
The game can also be played on a chalkboard or white board, using colored chalk or markers. The child draws a ball on the tree when he answers correctly.

Craft: Manger Diorama

Cut brown construction paper into four equal rectangles. Fold each one as shown, to make a manger. Ask children what letter the manger looks like when held lengthwise. Give a manger to each child.

Let children put small pieces of craft hay or yellow paper strips in the middle of the manger.

Glue two cotton balls together. Use a marker to make dots for the eyes and mouth on the "face." Give one to each child to place in her manger.

Game: Marshmallow–Throwing Contest

Give each child two large marshmallows. With two tries each, children take turns seeing who can throw the farthest. Then have everyone start at the same time and see who can pick up the most marshmallows from the floor. Pass out new marshmallows to eat.

Variation:
Aim the marshmallows at a target–a box or basket. Children will also enjoy holding a small box or basket and trying to catch marshmallows thrown by another child.

Ideas to Reinforce the Letters *M* and *N* and Number *7*

Give each child seven candy-coated chocolates. Show how to lay them out, forming a number 7. Then eat.

Have children draw large letters *M* and *N* on the chalkboard.

Serve **m**ints, **m**acaroons, **m**ilk, or **m**elon balls rolled in crushed **n**uts

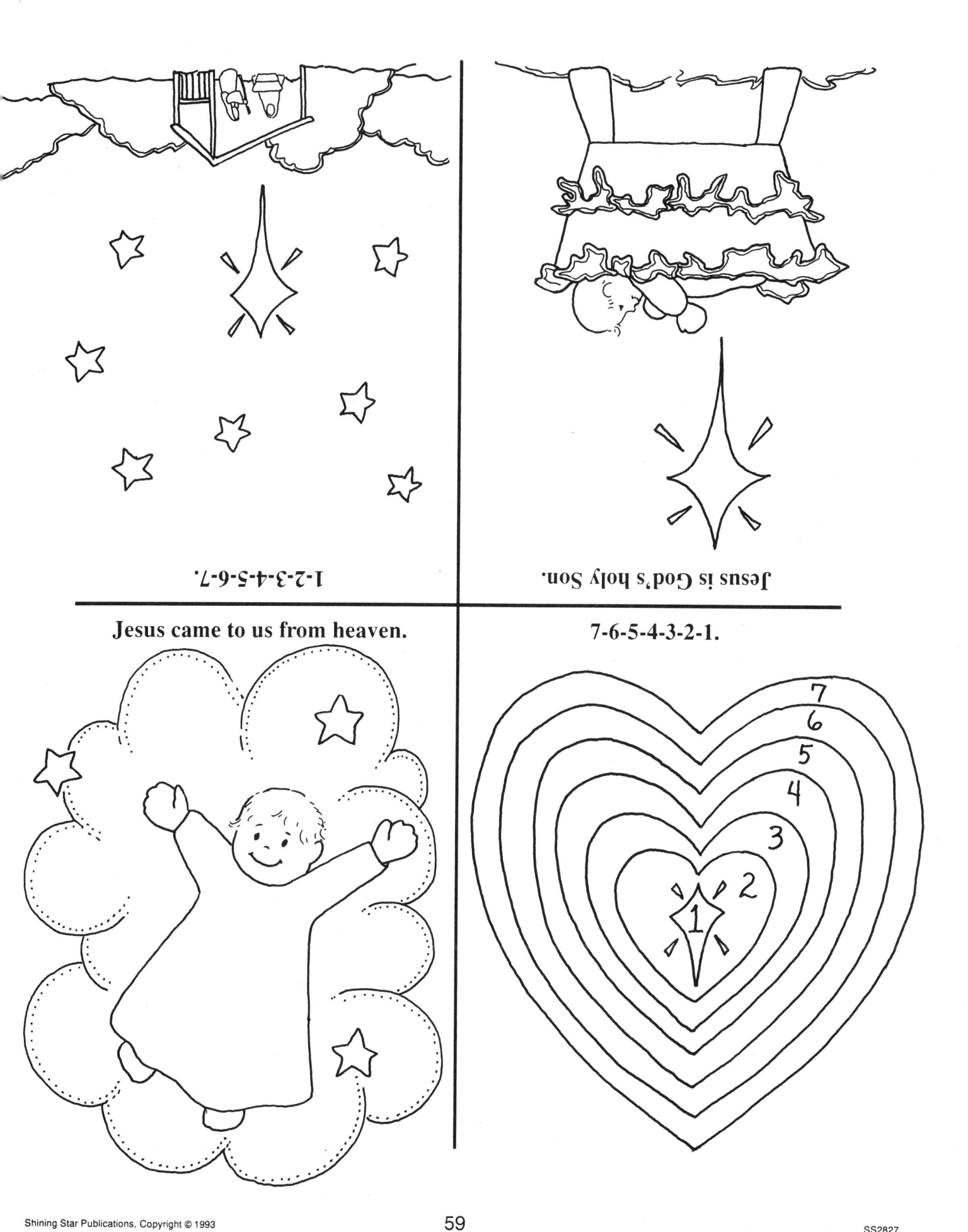

Fold on dotted lines to make a mini book about counting to seven.

Jesus came to us from heaven.

1-2-3-4-5-6-7.

Jesus is God's holy Son.

7-6-5-4-3-2-1.

Chapter 8

O is for Oval. *P* is for Peter.

Peter Followed Jesus
Tune: "Peter, Peter, Pumpkin-Eater"

Peter, Peter followed Jesus when He came from God above.

Peter, Peter learned from Jesus how to live and walk in love.

(Optional Tune: "Reuben and Rachel")

Finger Play About Peter
(Luke 5:1-11)
(With refrain after each verse, this can be sung to the tune "This Old Man.")

In the boat. In the boat.	*(Cup hands, forming a boat; rock gently side to side.)*
Peter fishing in the boat.	

(Refrain)
And what Jesus says,
We quickly will obey;
We will do it right away.

In the net. In the net.	*(Draw a pretend net to self, hand over hand.)*
Caught no fishes in the net.	*(Shake head no.)*
Try again. Try again.	*(Cup hands to mouth as if shouting.)*
Jesus tells them, "Try again."	
In the net. In the net.	*(Draw net again. Sling it over shoulder.)*
All the fish are in the net.	
Thank the Lord. Thank the Lord.	*(Palms together, head bowed.)*
Peter stops to thank the Lord.	

P is for Peter.

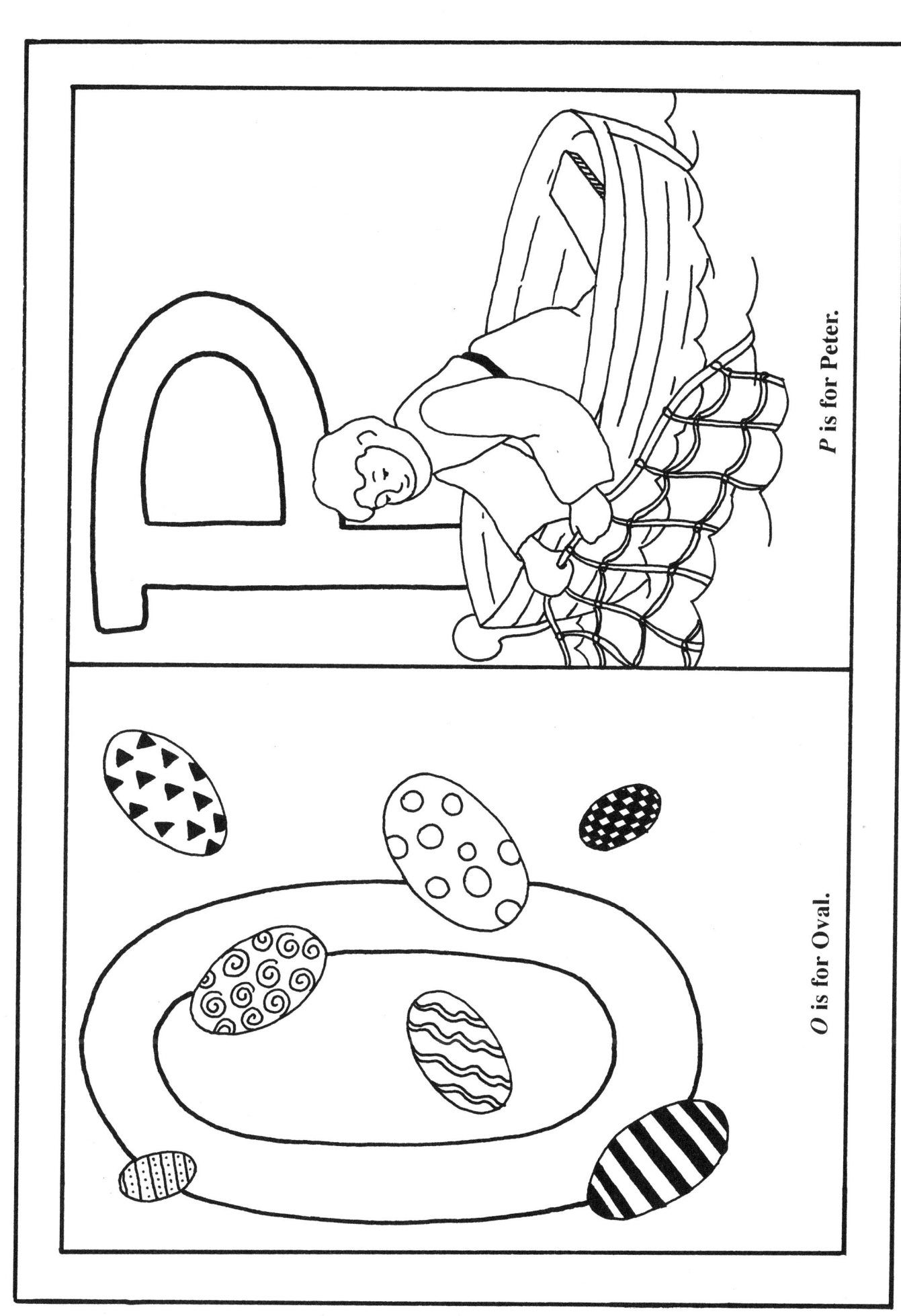

O is for Oval.

Color the frame pink.

Color and Number Fun: Eight Pink Pigs

Show children which crayon or marker is pink. Have them color the frame on their alphabet picture. Some may choose to color in the oval also.

Ask: What color are pigs usually? Here's an exercise about eight pink pigs they will enjoy.

Select eight children (or eight pink crayons or strips of pink paper) to be pigs. When the rhyme calls for counting, have "pigs" step forward as they are counted.

Eight pink pigs learn how to skate. 1-2-3-4-5-6-7-8.

Eight pink pigs go on a date. 1-2-3-4-5-6-7-8.

Eight pink pigs go in the gate. 1-2-3-4-5-6-7 WAIT!

One is late; he's stuck in the gate.

Here he comes—8!

(If children are the "pigs," they could wear pink paper hats.) Discuss the color pink and the sound of the letter *P*. Talk about the words that rhyme with *eight*.

For a treat, serve strawberry ice cream, pink lemonade, or red gelatin made with whipped cream topping added to make it pink.

Phonics Skill: *O* Sounds

The letter *O* has more than one sound. One sound is the first one you hear in the word *open*. Another sound is the first one you hear in the word *off*.

Eye-Hand Coordination: Drawing Ovals

The teacher can draw on the chalkboard while saying this rhyme. Then repeat it slowly while children draw on the chalkboard, on paper, or in the air. (Emphasize the O sound in the words *oval* and *over*.)

I can draw ovals over and over.	*(Do so.)*
I can draw letter *O*, too.	*(Draw large O.)*
I can draw circles over and over.	*(Do so.)*
I can draw *8* for you.	*(Put one circle on top of another to make 8.)*

Discuss things shaped like an oval, and have some of them on hand for children to see (eggs, place mats, bowl of a spoon, the head on a stick figure).

Cut various-sized ovals and circles from pink construction paper. Mix them together on a table top or floor. Let children take turns picking up a shape and telling whether it is a circle or an oval. Mix them up again, and have children take turns picking up the shape named by the teacher.

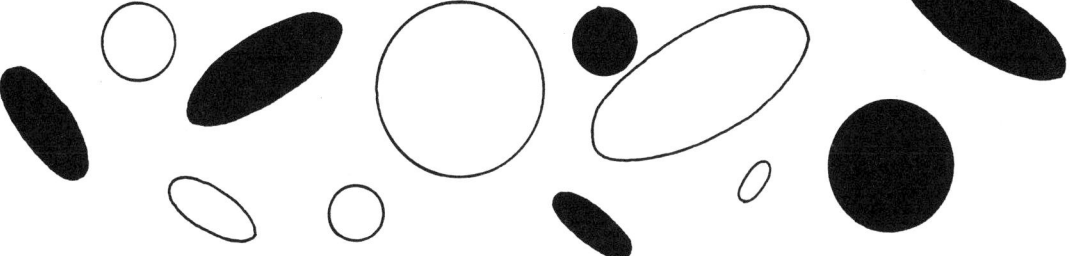

Learning Spatial Relationships

Use a box, a table, and one other object or toy. Place these three items in various positions and state the relationship. Then have children do the same. See the following examples:

The doll is in the box.
The box is under the table.
The table is on the floor.

Include these spatial relationships: next to, in front of, behind, beside.

Then give each child a strand of pink yarn, one yard long. Help each one form an oval on the floor with his yarn. Then give directions such as the following:

Stand in front of the oval.
Stand in the oval.
Put your feet outside the oval.
Put one hand on the yarn.

Let's Pretend

Let's pretend we are going fishing in a boat. What kind of boat will it be? Let's pretend it's a canoe. Everyone hold the paddle and row like this. (Row with both arms on the same side of a pretend canoe.)

We can have a motorboat now. Pull the rope to start the motor. (Do so.) Here we go. Hold on to your hat. Now you can turn your boat by using the steering wheel, just like driving a car. (Pretend to steer.)

Now we can pretend we're in a rowboat. Hold the oars like this and row with both arms. (Demonstrate.) Now walk backwards, because that's the way a rowboat goes.

We can pretend we're in a sailboat now. This is the way you move the sails. (Look up and pretend to manipulate a rope.)

When Peter went fishing, he probably had a rowboat or a boat with sails. Instead of using a fishing pole, he threw a net into the water and pulled it up again. Let's pretend to throw a net over the side of our boat. (Do so.) Now pull it back into the boat. Did you catch any fish? Let's count how many fish we caught. (Count to eight.)

Net-Fishing Game

Materials:
large basin such as a baby's bathtub or a vegetable drawer from a refrigerator
twenty to forty small fish shapes cut from one-fourth-inch foam
twelve-inch-square piece of nylon net or mesh vegetable bag

Fill basin half-full of water and add the foam fish. Agitate the water a little. Let children take turns "fishing" with the net. Count the fish each child catches.

Craft: Pudding Paint

Mix instant pudding with more water than called for. (It should be the consistency of finger paint.) Put a small glob of pudding on a large piece of waxed paper or freezer wrap. Lay a sheet of waxed paper on top. Let children work on the top sheet making designs between the two sheets.

Craft: Oval Ornaments

Cut uniform ovals out of construction paper, two of each of the colors the children have learned. Cut a line halfway through each oval, as shown. Mix up the ovals, and let children match the colored ovals. Slide ovals together at the slits to make a decoration. They can be taken apart and used again. When ornaments are ready to be hung, open a paper clip, and puncture one of the ovals. Hang on a string or a Christmas tree.

This exercise can also be done with paper cut in circles, triangles, and squares.

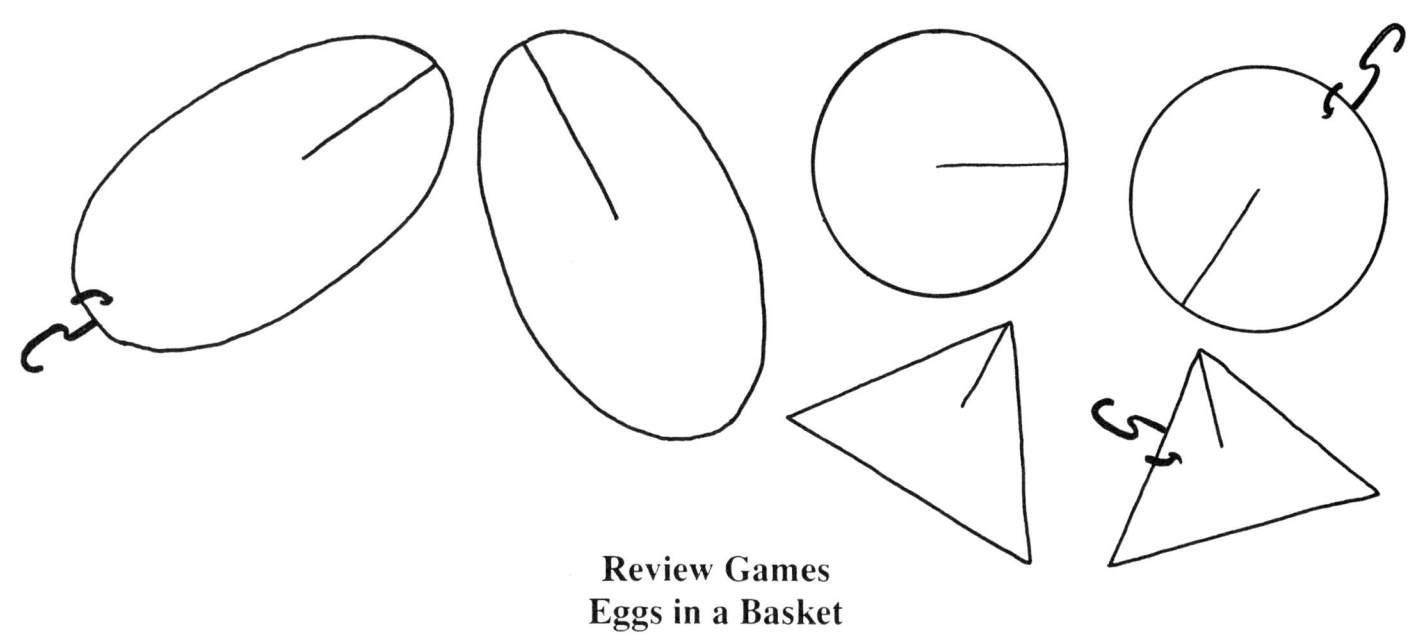

Review Games
Eggs in a Basket

Use this game to review anything the children have been learning. Draw a large basket on the board. When children get a correct answer, they come to the board and draw an oval (egg) in the basket.

If the game is played with teams, draw a basket for each team. At the end, see which team has the most eggs in their basket.

Pumpkin Pie

Draw a large circle on the board. Tell the children it is a pumpkin pie. Help them hear the sound the letter *P* makes.

Draw a line through the center to divide the "pie" in half, and have the children count the pieces.

Draw another line and count to four. Continue until the pie has been divided into eight pieces.

Seatwork

Reproduce this number exercise for each child. Have him trace the numbers. Suggestion: A pink crayon or marker could be used.

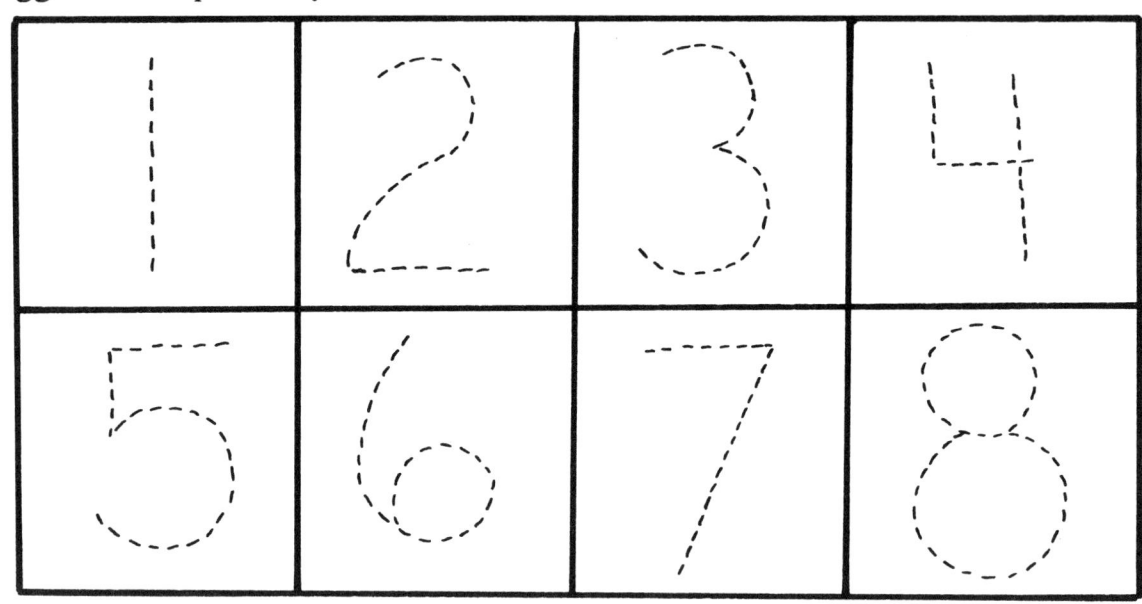

1	2	3	4
5	6	7	8

Ideas to Reinforce the Letters *O* and *P*
Pink Popcorn Ovals
(Microwave Recipe)

1 cup brown sugar
1 stick margarine
$1/4$ c. white corn syrup
$1/2$ tsp. salt
1 tsp. vanilla
red food color
$1/2$ tsp. baking soda
4-5 qts. popped corn

Combine all ingredients except soda and popcorn in 2-qt. baking dish. Bring to a boil in microwave. Then microwave on full power for 2 minutes.
Remove from oven and stir in soda.

Put popped corn in a large brown grocery bag. Pour syrup over popcorn. Close bag and shake well. Cook bag in microwave for $1^1/_2$ minutes on high. Shake bag and cook another 1-2 minutes. Pour out and form into ovals. (Wear buttered plastic bags on your hands to do this.)

Peanut Butter Ovals
(Children can make this recipe.)

Mix equal parts honey, peanut butter, and powdered milk. Form into ovals. (Optional: Roll balls in sprinkles, chopped nuts, or coconut.)

Letters and Numbers

Form letters and numbers using cereal or pretzel sticks.

Fold on lines to make a mini book about Peter.

Peter, Peter followed Jesus

how to live and walk in love.

when He came from God above.

Peter, Peter learned from Jesus

Chapter 9

Q is for Queen. *R* is for Red.

Esther's People
Tune: "Glory, Glory, Hallelujah"

Esther's people were in danger. *(Hands shield eyes, looking around.)*
Esther's people were in danger.
Esther's people were in danger,
  But what could Esther do?

Bravely, Esther held a banquet. *(Act out eating motions.)*
Bravely, Esther held a banquet.
Bravely, Esther held a banquet
  To ask the king for help.

So the king gave her a promise. *(Shake hands with each other.)*
So the king gave her a promise.
So the king gave her a promise.
  Her people would be saved.

Every year there's celebration. *(Pump fist in air.)*
Every year there's celebration.
Every year there's celebration,
  'Cause Esther saved the Jews.

Number Fun: Three-in-a-Row Bingo

Create bingo cards by dividing squares of paper into nine boxes. Put numbers 1 through 9 randomly in the boxes. Give a bingo card to each child.

Write numbers 1 through 9 on cards, and lay them facedown. Turn them over one at a time, calling out the number.

Children cover that number on their paper with a penny, button, or small square of paper.

When someone covers three in a row, he shouts "Bingo," and the game starts over.

7	3	5
4	6	1
2	9	8

R is for Red.

Q is for Queen.

Color the frame red.

Color Fun: Red

Show children which crayon or marker is red. Instruct them to color the frame around their alphabet picture red. Some children may wish to color the queen's robe and the crayon on their alphabet picture red.

Ask every child who is wearing something red to stand and show it to the class. Acknowledge it by saying "Timmy's shirt has red on it, Amber's socks are red," etc.

Ask the following:
"What color is lipstick?
What color are some apples?
What color are cherries?
What color are ripe tomatoes?
What color is our tongue?
What color are some roses?
What color is blood?"

(If possible, show the children a red lipstick, a red apple, maraschino cherries, a red tomato, and a red flower, or pictures of them.)

You may want to have a "Red Day" when everyone wears or brings something red.

For a treat, serve red punch with red apple slices, maraschino cherries, or tomato wedges sprinkled with sugar.

Finger Play: The Red Robe

The Queen wears a red robe.	*(Hold up index finger. Circle it at the base with your other hand.)*
She is royalty.	*(Hold up index finger tall and straight.)*
She rides in a chariot.	*(Hold other hand under the queen hand, and bump it along as if riding.)*
The people treat her royally.	*(Make fingers on other hand bow slowly to the queen finger.)*

Finger Play: Number Review

Hold up nine fingers. Drop a finger on the second line of each verse.

There were nine in a line, waiting for a train.
One gave up and took a plane.
There were eight at the gate, waiting for the plane.
One started walking down a lane.
Then there were seven, walking down a lane.
One turned back when it started to rain.
There were six in a fix, walking in the rain.
One fell down and got a sprain.
There were five all alive, without a sprain.
One decided to go to Spain.
There were four at the door, going into Spain.
One was a queen with a long, red train.
There were three having tea near the queenly train.
One spilled his cup and made a stain.
There were two like you, wiping up the stain.
One went away to look for Jane.
Then there was one, whose name was Jane.
She decided to take a train.

Phonics Skill

Ask children to listen for the sounds of the letter *R* in the following sentences:
Ride a **r**aft on the **R**ed **R**iver.
The **r**ed **r**abbit **r**uns **r**apidly ove**r** the **r**ocks.

Play this phonics game called Quick Commands.

Tell children you are going to say words with *Q* in them. They will do what the word indicates until you say "Quit." (You are to do the action, also, to show them how.)

quack	quiver	squat
quake	squint	quiet
squeak	squirm	

(Don't say "Quit" after the last one!)

Let's Pretend

Let all the girls pretend to be Queen Esther. Show the motions so children can imitate you. Let all the boys pretend to be the king. Repeat with appropriate actions.

1. Esther put on her red robe.
2. Esther put on pretty makeup.
3. Esther put on her favorite perfume.
4. Esther put on a necklace, bracelet, rings, and anklet.
5. Esther put on her crown.
6. Esther went to the king. *(Prance around the room.)*
7. Esther bowed to the king.
8. The king was kind to Esther. *(Use no motions.)*

Seatwork: Rubbings

Remove paper from several used crayons. Show children how to lay paper over an object and rub it with the side of a crayon until the shape of the object appears.

Try this with coins, fresh leaves, a small square of nylon net, kite string, or shapes cut out of cardstock paper.

Craft: Queen Esther's Necklace

Each child will need a length of red yarn, O-shaped cereal, small macaroni, and pasta wheels. (You may want to spray the pasta ahead of time with gold and silver paint).

Show children how to thread the pasta and cereal onto the yarn. When a child is satisfied with her necklace, tie it around her neck.

Bracelets and anklets can also be made.

Review Game

Divide your group into several teams, and assign a color to each team. Use colors the children have learned, including red.

Put five-to-ten colored chalk marks on the board for each team. When someone on the team answers correctly, he erases one mark of his team's color.

The first team to erase all its marks is the winner.

Game: King, King, Queen
(Like "Duck, Duck, Goose")

This game can be played indoors on chairs or on the floor, or outdoors on the grass.

Children sit in a circle. One child who is "It" goes up and down the rows tapping each sitting child on the head and saying "King."

Sometimes "It" says "Queen" instead. The child chosen as Queen chases after "It" and tries to tag him. "It" tries to sit in the Queen's chair before being tagged.

If "It" is tagged by the Queen, he is "It" again. If "It" gets to the Queen's chair first, the Queen becomes "It."

Game: Drop the Hanky

Children stand in a circle. The child who is "It" goes around the outside of the circle holding a red hanky. "IT" drops the hanky behind someone's feet. Then the person with the hanky at his feet must chase and try to tag "It," who runs around the circle and tries to pick up the hanky before getting tagged. If "It" is successful, the child who chased "It" becomes "It." Otherwise, "It" goes again.

Ideas to Reinforce the Letters *Q* and *R* and the Color Red

Quick Ice Cream:
1 can evaporated milk, chilled in a freezer
1 6 oz. can frozen orange juice concentrate
1 cup sugar

Whip the milk until fluffy. Add sugar and orange juice concentrate until well blended. Place in a freezer for two hours.

Use instant vanilla pudding colored with red food coloring as finger paint. Let the children practice forming the letters *Q* and *R* with the edible red paint.

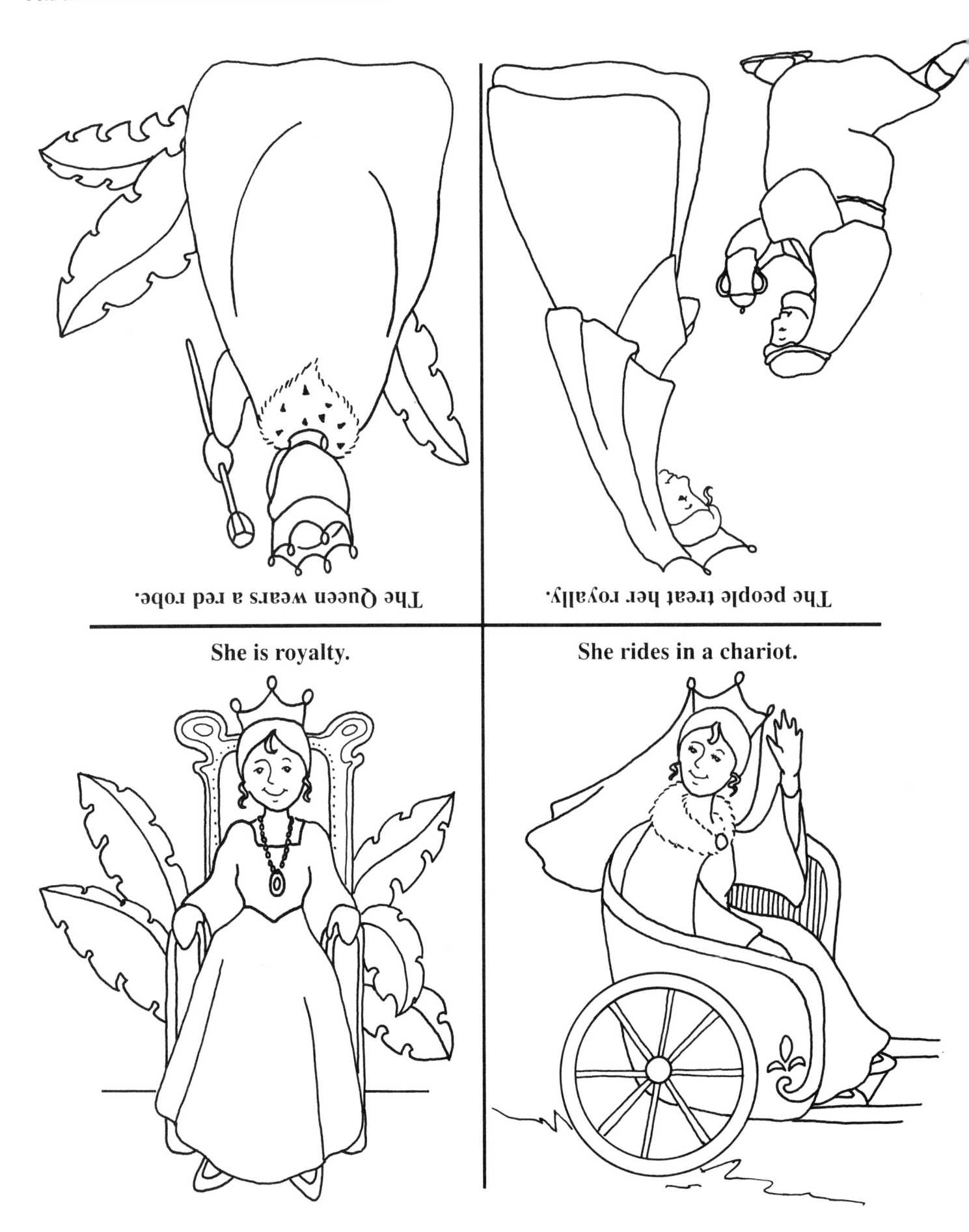

Fold on lines to make a mini book about the color red.

The Queen wears a red robe.

The people treat her royally.

She is royalty.

She rides in a chariot.

Chapter 10

S is for Samson.   **T is for Ten.**

Heroes for God
Tune: "Fishers of Men"

Samson was a hero for God,
  Hero for God,
  Hero for God.
Samson was a hero for God
When he kept God's Word.

(*For every line about heroes, make a muscle on one arm; feel it with the with the other hand.*)

  When he kept God's Word,
    When He kept God's Word–
Samson was a hero for God
When he kept God's Word.

(*For every line about God's Word, hold hands open like a book.*)

I can be a hero for God,
  Hero for God,
  Hero for God.
I can be a hero for God
When I keep God's Word.

  When I keep God's Word,
    When I keep God's Word–
I can be a hero for God
When I keep God's Word.

Samson Was Strong
Tune: "Row, Row, Row Your Boat"
Samson was strong when his hair was long
and when he did what was right.
I am strong when I don't do wrong
and when I do what is right.

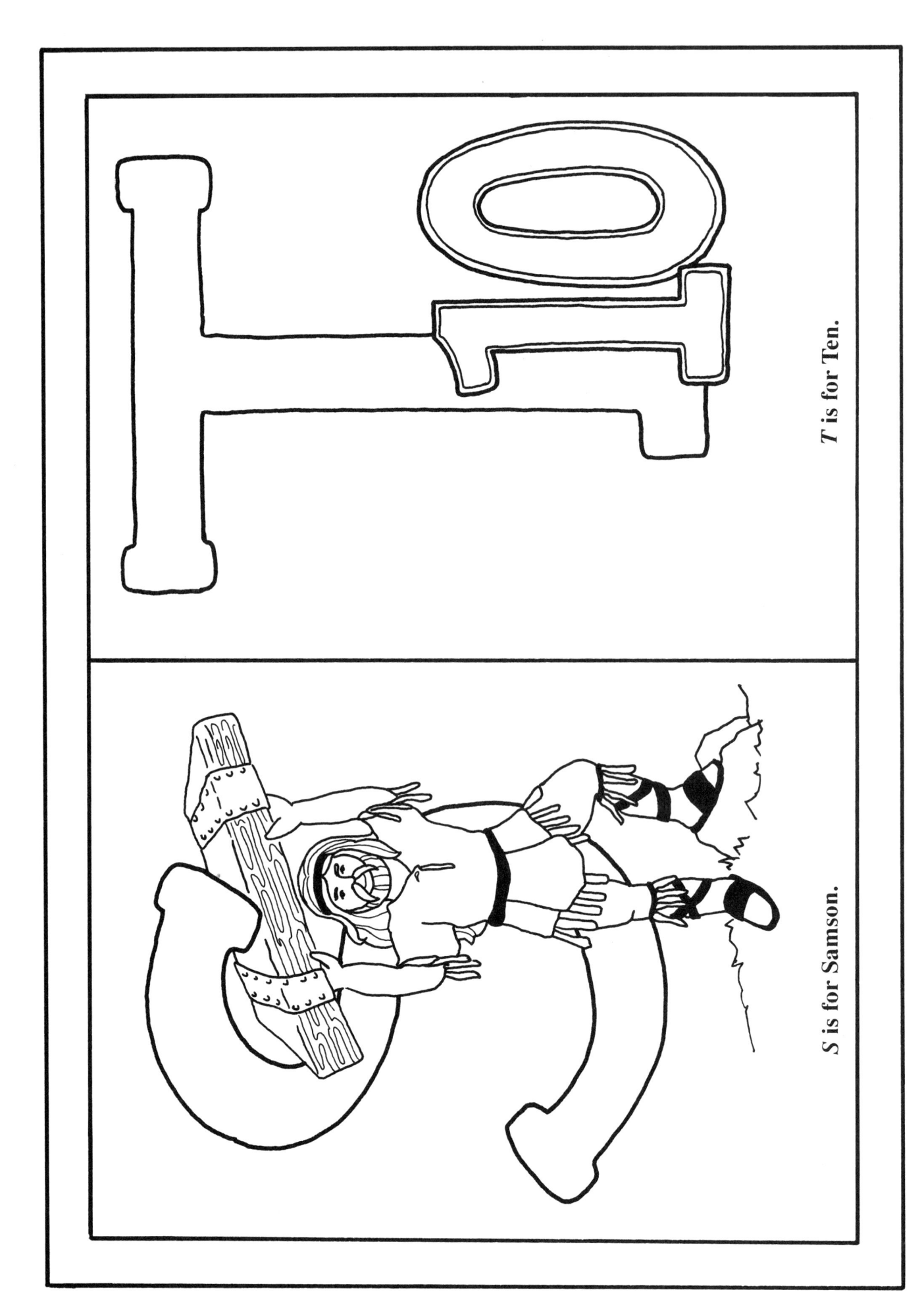

T is for Ten.

S is for Samson.

Color the frame your favorite color.

Shining Star Publications. Copyright © 1993

SS2827

Number Fun: Finger People
Tune: "Ten Little Indians"

Draw eyes (two dots) and a smiling mouth on every child's fingertips. The teacher holds up the correct number of fingers as the song progresses. Children will imitate as best they can.

One little, two little, three little fingers,
Four little, five little, six little fingers,
Seven little, eight little, nine little fingers,
  Ten little finger people.

Hit 'em together and hear them clapping.   *(Clap hands.)*
Hit 'em together and hear them clapping.
Hit 'em together and hear them clapping.
  Ten little finger people.

Put 'em together and see them praying.   *(Put hands together in praying*
Put 'em together and see them praying.   *position.)*
Put 'em together and see them praying.
  Ten little finger people.

Fold 'em together and they are sleeping.   *(Fold hands, fingers intertwined.)*
Fold 'em together and they are sleeping.
Fold 'em together and they are sleeping.
  Ten little finger people.

Finger Play: Ten Little Fingers

Ten little fingers standing in a row—	*(Hold all fingers up.)*
They bow to the King and Queen just so.	*(Bend fingers slowly.)*
They walk to the left.	*(Move hands to the left.)*
They walk to the right.	*(Move hands to the right.)*
They clap, clap, clap,	*(Clap three times.)*
And say, "Good night."	*(Wave bye-bye.)*

Other Songs to Sing and a Rhyme to Say:
"There Were Ten in a Bed, and the Little One Said, "Roll Over"
"The Ants Go Marching One by One"
"One, Two, Buckle My Shoe"

Color Fun: Color Review Games

Children color one craft stick with each of the colors they have learned.

When the teacher calls out a color, the children hold up that stick. Children can do the calling also.

For practice in following instructions, tell children to lay the blue stick down, making it look like the number one. Add the orange stick to make a tepee. A green stick makes a triangle. The purple stick makes it a box. The grey stick can make it a house. Add the black stick for a rectangle. To make digital eight add the brown stick. The pink stick makes two diamonds. The red one makes a sparkler. (The teacher will need to show, as well as tell, the children what to do. Practice counting the sticks after each addition.)

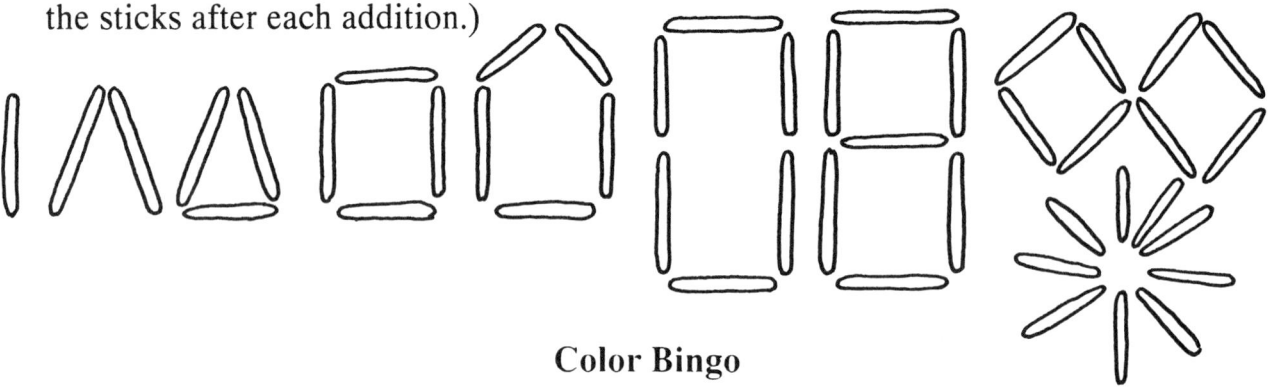

Color Bingo

Give each child a paper you have marked into nine equal spaces and colored randomly with the nine different colors the children have learned. Play like Number Bingo, page 68, until someone gets three in a row.

Colored Triangles

Divide a paper plate into nine sections. Using the nine colors the children have learned, color each wedge a different color. Fasten a spinner in the center with a brad. Children take turns spinning and naming the color indicated. (Optional: Instead of a spinner, a pinch clothespin can be used to indicate a color the child is to name.)

Balloon Review

From a party supply store, buy balloons in each of the nine colors the children have learned. Without looking, a child pulls a balloon out of a bag. If he can name the color correctly, he keeps the balloon. If he is incorrect, he puts the balloon back and tries again.

What Is Missing?

Use eighteen spools of thread, two of each of the colors learned. Place them all on a table top. All children turn their backs while one spool is taken away. Children turn around and figure out which color is missing. Repeat until children tire of the game. (Let children take turns removing the spool.)

Let's Pretend: A Carnival of Choices

Note to teacher:
This object lesson takes some advance preparation. Use small paper cups.

In one cup put sugar; in another put salt.
Fill one with soda pop and another with chocolate-flavored water.
Fill one with water and another with white vinegar.
Squirt shaving cream in one and canned whipped cream in another.
Put popcorn seeds in one and small gravel in another. Improvise a lid for them (or use empty 35 mm film cases).

Samson had to make some difficult choices in his life. Some were right, and God was pleased. Some were wrong and didn't please God.

Let's pretend we have some choices to make. Without smelling or touching these cups, see if you can tell which is sugar and which is salt. If you're wrong, your cereal is going to taste awful.

Continue with each set of cups until children recognize how difficult some decisions are. We cannot always decide by how things look or feel. Emphasize that we must choose what is right even if what is wrong looks the same or better.

Physical Exercise

See who can do some of the following actions ten times:
Hop up and down/Sit and stand/March ten steps/Clap ten times/
Nod your head/Raise your arms/Wiggle your "tail"/
Make a muscle ten times/Touch your toes/Lift one leg

Phonics Skill: Listen for the Sound

Repeat words that begin with *S* and *T* emphasizing the beginning sound. Let children say the sound or letter they hear. If children respond well, review other letters *A* . . . *R*.

Finger Play: This Is Ten

See Finger Play: This Is One on page 37, and add these lines:
This is six. *Do some kicks.*
This is seven. *Point to heaven.*
This is eight. *Stand up straight.*
This is nine. *Get in line.*
This is ten. *The end!*

Games: Match the Lid

Collect lids from gallon jugs, ten for each child and the teacher. Have several colors if possible. Mark each lid with a numeral 1 through 10. Try to have all the 1's orange, all the 2's blue, etc.

Children sit around a table or in a circle, each with ten lids. The teacher puts a lid in the center. The first child who matches the number by putting his lid in the center gets to keep both lids. (Have blank lids available in case of a tie.)

When all ten lids have been collected, divide the lids again, with each child making sure he has all ten numbers. Repeat the game. Perhaps the child who got the most lids could replace the teacher.

Fun with Toothpicks

Each child needs the following:
ten large marshmallows
fifty-five round toothpicks (color optional)
small cup of water

Wet one toothpick and stick it in the first marshmallow. Wet two toothpicks and stick them in the second marshmallow. Continue until the tenth marshmallow has ten toothpicks.

If children are too young for this, make it a group activity with teacher supervision. Children take turns working on one set of ten marshmallows.

Ideas to Reinforce the Letters *S* and *T*

Form letters *S* and *T* from any of the following before eating:
sunflower seeds   strawberries
tuna squares (tuna salad on square crackers)   tomato slices

Before eating, practice counting and name the foods that are red.

Fold on lines to make a mini book about Samson.

Samson was strong when his hair was long

and when I do what is right.

and when he did what was right.

I am strong when I don't do wrong

Chapter 11

U is for Us.

W is for White.

V is for Vowels.

I Can Sing the Vowels
Tune: "B-I-N-G-O"

I can sing the vowels, and I can write them, too.
   A–E–I–O–U   *(Teacher sings the five vowels in order.)*
   A–E–I–O–U   *(Repeat.)*
   A–E–I–O–U   *(Repeat.)*
I can sing the vowels.

Second verse: Instead of singing *A*, the teacher writes *A* on the board every time. Children either hum or clap it.

Third verse: Write *A* and *E*.
Fourth verse: Write *AEI*.
Fifth verse: Write *AEIO*.
Sixth verse: Write *AEIOU*.

Eventually children will be able to do the writing, too.

Note to teacher:
There is no Bible character in this chapter, but we can live for God just as Bible men and women did. This lesson will be about us.

W is for White.

V is for Vowels.

U is for Us.

Color the frame white.

Number Fun and Color Fun

Give each child eleven cotton balls in a paper cup or other container. Say a number, and have children lay that number of balls on the table. Repeat randomly with numbers one through eleven.

What Is White?
Tune: "Twinkle, Twinkle, Little Star"

White is cotton; white is snow.
We see white clouds high and low.
White is sugar, salt, and milk.
Brides wear white gowns made of silk.
White is cotton; white is snow.
What is white? Well, now we know.

For a treat, serve white bread or angel food cake and milk.

Body Awareness

I see with my _____.   (eyes)

I walk with my _____.   (feet)

I smell things with my _____.   (nose)

I chew with my _____.   (teeth)

I hear with my _____.   (ears)

I hold things with my _____.   (arms)

I smile with my _____.   (lips)

I swallow with my _____.   (tongue or throat)

I button clothes with my _____. (fingers)

I talk with my _____.   (mouth)

I clap with my _____.   (hands)

(Applaud yourselves.)

Letter Recognition

Show children how to make two *V*'s with the index finger and middle finger on both hands. Then put hands together to make a *W*.

Do it again while saying this rhyme:
> I can make the letter *V*.
> Now a *W* is what I see.

Make a *V* with your arms over your head. Then join with someone else to make a *W*. Say the rhyme again.

Then sit on the floor and make a *V* by spreading your legs. Move next to someone else to make it a *W*. Do it while saying the rhyme a third time.

Game: Beginning-Sound Track

This game can be played indoors or out, but if it is indoors, a large empty room is preferred.

On three posters make large letters, one for *U*, one for *V*, and one for *W*. Hang these on three different walls in the room. If outside, lay them on the ground in three different locations (for example, west, south, and east) but all facing toward the middle.

Children stand in a group in the middle of the area. Tell them to listen for the beginning sound of the words you will name. If the children hear the *U* sound, they should all run to the *U* poster and wait for the next word. If they hear the *W* sound, they should run to the *W* poster, and so on.

This game emphasizes whole-body exercise and energy use as well as listening skills.

Word List:

us	white	vowel	wash	up	vase
wait	umpire	valve	web	vine	uphill
weed	walnut	van	unreal	we	vein
voice	way	view	unfold	vest	weird
week	warm	under	vacuum	wet	ulcer
west	view	visit	unload	worm	upset
weather	upstairs	uncle	winners	umbrella	

Game: Musical Chairs

Have one chair per child, and a letter card on each chair. (Include *U, V, W* and letters children may be having trouble with.) Children march around chairs until the music stops. Then each child picks up a letter and sits down. Children take turns naming the letters they are holding. When all letters have been named, place the cards back on the chairs and repeat the game.

Variation #1:
Take away one chair, and repeat the game. The child left standing must go around and name all the letters.

Variation #2:
Children sit in a circle and pass the cards until the music stops. Then each child names the letter she is holding, and the game begins again.

Auditory Skill: Musical Tones

Fill six uniform glasses with different amounts of water. Count the glasses. Tap each glass lightly with a spoon and talk about the different tones. Help children distinguish between low and high tones. If there is a piano in the room, try to match the tones of the glasses with notes on the piano. (A simple toy xylophone may also be used.)

If real crystal goblets are available, use six of them filled with differing amounts of water. Wet your finger and run it around the rim of each goblet until it "sings."

Sensory Skill: The Nose Knows

Put each of the following objects in a separate lunch bag, and pinch the top to a very small opening:

cinnamon sticks
dried flower potpourri
orange sections
corn chips
unwrapped mint-type gum

bar of soap
vanilla extract on a cotton ball
after-shave on a cotton ball
dry dog food
round lid with toothpaste in it

First ask children to smell the contents and decide whether or not they could be eaten. Put "edible" bags in one place, and "non-food" bags in another, according to what the children decide.

Then taking one bag at a time, let various children smell and guess what is in it, until someone guesses correctly. Then discuss whether or not it is edible. (Be sure children know the meaning of *edible*.)

Did their noses fool them, or were they correct most of the time? Discuss why God gave us noses.

Game: Imitate the Leader

Count to eleven. Ask who can do something eleven times. For example, "Who can jump up and down eleven times?" As a child does so, say "Do you see what (child's name) can do? See if you can do it, too." Then have every child try it while you count to eleven.

Craft: Paper Plate Masks

Hold a white paper plate up to each child's face and mark eyes. Cut out eye circles. Let the children decorate with crayons or markers. If they are able, they may glue yarn pieces on for hair. Punch a hole on each side or staple yarn to each side, so the plate can be tied around the child's head.

Let's Pretend: Bible Character Review

Have children wear their plate masks and pretend to be Bible characters. Ask who they are and what they did. (You may need to ask Yes and No questions.)

Craft: Self-Awareness

Use a roll of wide paper such as newsprint, butcher paper, or freezer paper.

Have each child lie down on paper, and trace around him with a marker. The child will enjoy seeing himself in outline. The form can be cut out and designed with features to look like the child.

Ideas to Reinforce the Letters *U, V,* and *W*

unique waffles (Put raisins in the squares to make the number 11. Pour on syrup, and enjoy.)
vanilla wafers
vegetable-flavored crackers
wheat-flavored crackers
With clean hands, form letters and do counting exercises with the wafers or crackers before eating.

Fold on lines to make a mini book about the vowels.

I can sing the vowels,

I can sing the vowels,

and I can write them, too.

A, E, I, O, U

Chapter 12

X is for eXercise.   Y is for Yellow.
Z is for Zacchaeus.

Zacchaeus Finds the Lord
Tune: "We Are Climbing Jacob's Ladder"

In the . . . tree sits . . . small Zacchaeus.   *(Shade eyes with hand.)*
In the . . . tree sits . . . small Zacchaeus.
In the . . . tree sits . . . small Zacchaeus
  Watching . . . for the . . . Lord.

Jesus . . . looks up . . . at Zacchaeus.   *(Look up, still shading eyes.)*
Jesus . . . looks up . . . at Zacchaeus.
Jesus . . . looks up . . . at Zacchaeus
  Waiting . . . for the . . . Lord.

Jesus . . . says, "Come . . . down, Zacchaeus."   *(Motion with finger, still looking up.)*
Jesus . . . says, "Come . . . down, Zacchaeus."
Jesus . . . says, "Come . . . down, Zacchaeus.
  I will . . . be your . . . Lord."

Finger Play About Zacchaeus

Zacchaeus was small.   *(Measure with hand close to the floor.)*
He was not tall.   *(Reach as high as you can.)*
And lo, he was a sinner!   *(Shake finger.)*

But Jesus is kind.
He wanted to find Zacchaeus   *(Shade eyes with hand, searching.)*
And take him to dinner.   *(Act out eating motions.)*

Now Zacchaeus is glad.   *(Point to smiling mouth.)*
He is not sad,   *(Shake head no.)*
And lo, he is a winner.   *(Pump air with fist.)*

X is for eXercise.

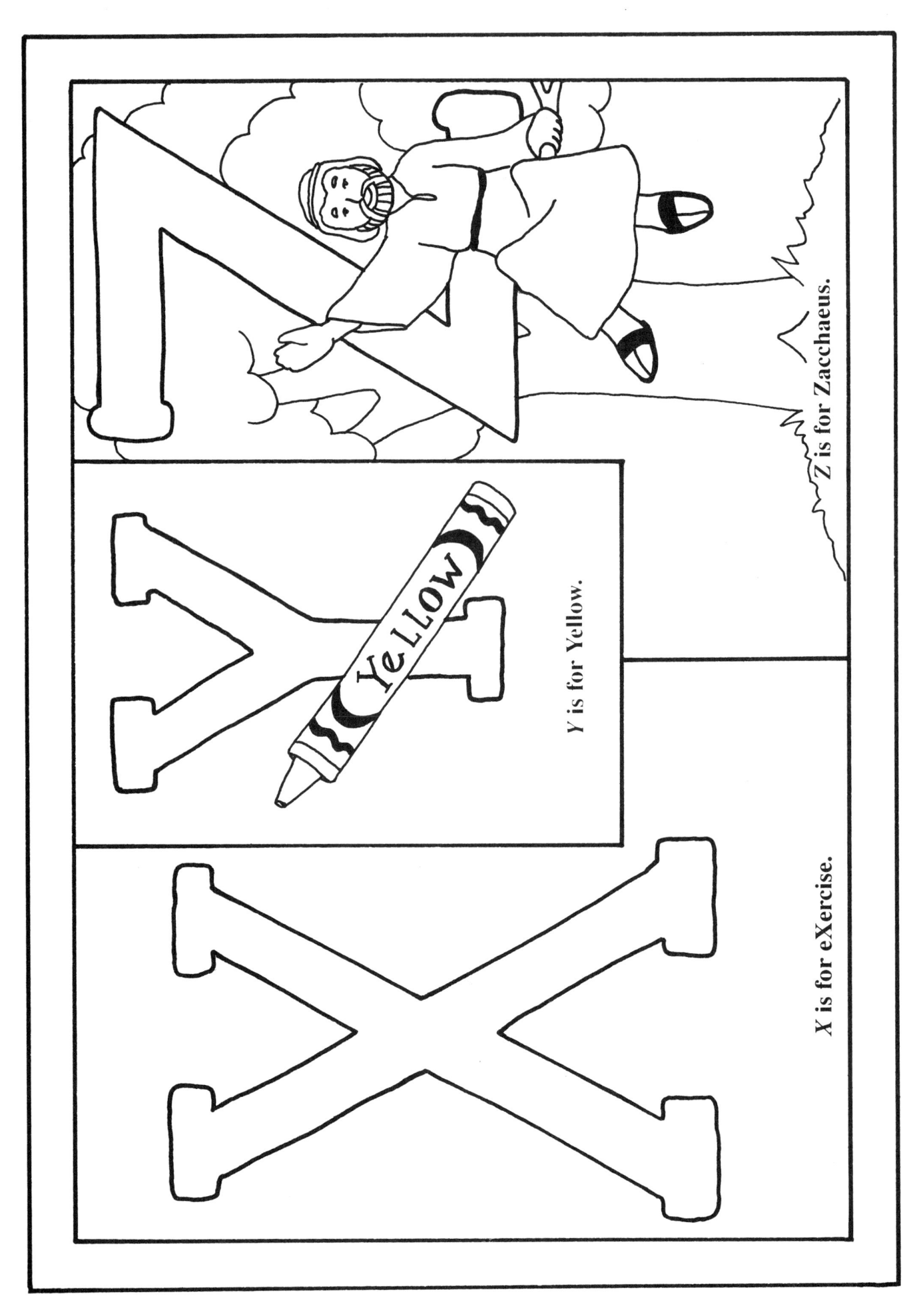

Y is for Yellow.

Z is for Zacchaeus.

Color the frame yellow.

Number Fun: Dominoes and Dice

From two to four players can play the traditional game of dominoes. Another way to play is to have players take turns selecting a domino and counting all the dots on it. Players put them in piles according to the total number of dots on each domino. This will be a good pre-math skill for the children.

See page 48 and improvise games with dice which will help the children in adding up to twelve. For example, choose a number between two and twelve. Let all children keep rolling their own two dice and counting the dots until they roll that number.

Number Practice

Each child has an open egg carton with dried beans in the lid section. Instruct the children to put one bean in one egg cup (it doesn't have to be the "first" egg cup). Put two beans in a different cup, etc., until the final cup holds twelve beans.

Discuss relationships, such as which cup has the most, which has the least, how many have few, how many have a lot.

Then take the twelve beans out and count them as they are put back into the lid. Do the same with eleven, etc., until all egg cups are empty again.

Color Fun: Yellow

Let children point out things that are yellow. Use yellow yarn to make a trail around the room. It can go under tables, over chairs, and through the halls. Have children follow the yellow-yarn trail. Serve lemonade, yellow candy, fruit juice bars, or suckers at the end of the trail.

Song About Yellow
Tune: "The Bear Went over the Mountain"

The yellow bird is a-flying (Sing three times.)   *(Flap arms.)*
  To take her young some food.

The yellow yarn is a-spinning (Sing three times.) *(Roll hands over each other.)*
  To make a coat of wool.

The yellow sun is a-shining (Sing three times.)   *(Clasp hands overhead forming*
  To make the flowers grow.   *a circle with arms.)*

The yellow bus is a-coming (Sing three times.)   *(Shade eyes with hand.)*
  To take the kids to school.

X is for eXercise: Preschool Olympics
Balancing Skill

Lay a 2 x 4 board on the floor. At first, hold the child's hand while she walks on the board. After she gains confidence, she can balance without help. Some will want to try walking it backwards or taking giant steps. Timid children can be encouraged to walk with one foot on the beam and one foot off.

Giant Steps

Mark off an area and record how many giant steps it takes each child to cover the area. You may want to try the same thing with bunny hops and walking backwards.

Broad Jump

This game should be played on sand or grass. Place two rulers 5" apart. Children line up behind each other. Each child jumps over the rulers and returns to the end of the line. When all have jumped, one ruler is moved 4-6" farther, and children jump again. When a child does not clear the rulers, he is out of the game. Continue until one child is left and declared the winner.

Hopping Contest

See how many times a child can hop on one foot without stopping. Record that number. Have play-offs to break ties.

Javelin Throw

Mark a line for children to stand behind. Each child throws a paper straw with his name or initials on it. The child throwing his straw the farthest wins. Repeat three times until you have three winners.

Awards Ceremony: For each event, give out yellow (gold=first place), grey (silver=second place), and brown (bronze=third place) medals cut from tagboard and hung on ribbons.

Children who do not win medals for the events can receive them for enthusiasm, sportsmanship, most improved, MVP, best effort, etc. Make sure all participants receive some type of award.

Tactile Exercise: Grab Bag
Place the following objects in a brown paper bag:

pencil	cloth strip
cotton ball	licorice stick
marble or bead	spool of thread
3" x 5" card	rubber ball
toy jack	a quarter

Without looking, a child reaches in the bag and tries to pull out the item you ask for. Discuss how he knew it was a pencil, cotton ball, etc. Help children distinguish various textures. How are the pencil and licorice stick alike and different? The marble and cotton ball? The card and the cloth?

(A younger child will need to look at the object he is searching for, so have two of each object–one for him to look at while searching for the other one in the bag.)

Variation:
Lay coins on a table–everything from pennies to half-dollars or silver dollars. Discuss how they are alike and different. Then put them in a bag, and see if children can pull out the smallest coin and the largest coin, by feeling and distinguishing them from each other.

Craft: Bookmark
Reproduce a bookmark for each child and discuss the choices Zacchaeus made before and after he met Jesus. Tell them the bookmark can remind them to make right choices.

Phonics Skill
Children will enjoy emphasizing the *Z* words in this rhyme:

I zip my zipper and zoom outside.

I zigzag up to you.

I'm as zany and full of zeal

As zebras in a zoo.

Let's Pretend: Action Story
(Luke 19:1-10)

Pause while children do the actions as you read this story:

Zacchaeus was so excited, he CLAPPED HIS HANDS. He had heard Jesus was coming to his town today, so he PUT ON HIS HAT and went outside.

He WALKED down the road until he came upon a large crowd of people. Everyone in town was STANDING UP TALL, waiting to see Jesus. No one would let Zacchaeus squeeze through, even though he MADE HIMSELF AS SKINNY AS POSSIBLE. That's because no one liked Zacchaeus. He was a mean man who took money from them.

Because Zacchaeus was very short, he couldn't see over the heads of the crowd. HE JUMPED UP HERE AND JUMPED UP THERE, but it was no use.

Zacchaeus STOMPED HIS FOOT in anger. "Now I'll never see Jesus!" he thought. Then he RUBBED HIS FOREHEAD and thought some more.

Suddenly, he had an idea. He LOOKED AROUND until he saw a sycamore tree. He RAN (run in place) to the tree and CLIMBED it. Zacchaeus CLIMBED HIGHER AND HIGHER until he could see out over the heads of all the people. He SAT on a limb and TOOK A DEEP BREATH.

Then the people began CHEERING AND WAVING. Jesus was coming down the road. Zacchaeus STOOD UP in the tree. As Jesus WALKED, the people parted and let Him through. Jesus KEPT WALKING until He was right under the tree where Zacchaeus was.

Jesus stopped and LOOKED UP at him. Jesus knew exactly what Zacchaeus needed. He said, "Come down from the tree, and I will go to your house."

Zacchaeus SCRAMBLED DOWN THE TREE as fast as he could. He took Jesus to his house, and they ate together. Then Zacchaeus said, "I'm sorry I've taken money from people. From now on, I'll give half of all my money to help the poor." Then Zacchaeus felt so happy, he LAUGHED OUT LOUD.

Ideas to Reinforce the Letters *X, Y,* and *Z*
eXtra Yummy Zucchini

Cut zucchini lengthwise and take out the seed portion. Cut into strips the size of large french fries. Make the letter *X* with two of the strips. Serve with dip.

yogurt
zwieback toast

Fold on lines to make a mini book about the letter Z.

I zip my zipper and zoom outside.

as zebras in a zoo.

I zigzag up to you.

I'm as zany and full of zeal

95

Activities for Letter and Number Review

Use alphabet-shaped cookies and crackers for review games and treats.

Writing Practice Box

Collect shallow, sturdy boxes, such as those in which chocolates are sold. If the box does not have a dark interior, glue dark construction paper to the bottom inside, making sure to seal the edges.

Fill the box with a layer of cornmeal approximately one-half inch deep. Children can practice writing numbers and letters in the cornmeal. Shake the box slightly to "erase." Store with the lid on.

Matching Game

Cut equal squares from heavy paper (3" x 5" cards cut in half will do). Make two cards for each number, letter, and color which has already been studied.

Arrange the cards facedown in neat rows. Children take turns turning over two cards so everyone can see the number, letter, or color. If they match, the child keeps them and takes another turn. If they don't match, the child turns them back over, and another child takes a turn. The child with the most matched cards at the end of the game is the winner. When adults are playing with young children, allow children to take double turns.

Dot Cards

For each set of dot cards, use twelve 3" x 5" cards with a line drawn across the middle. On one side write the number 1 through 12 as shown. On the other side draw that number of dots (or punch out that many holes). Use as flash cards by covering one half of the card, and letting the child say the number.

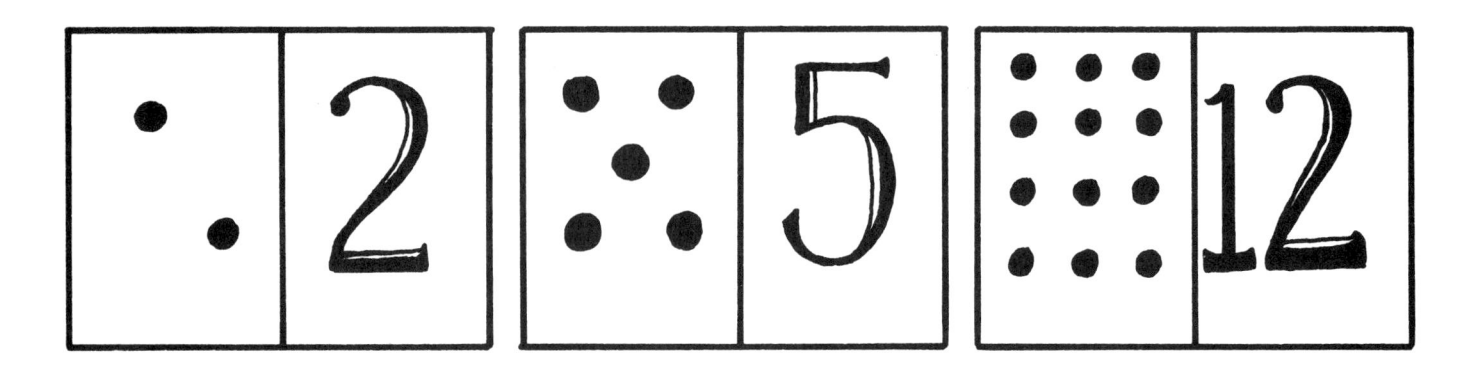

A variation that children can use by themselves consists of a set of twelve matchboxes. On the outside of the box, write the number. Inside place the corresponding number of objects, such as buttons, beans, or tiny cars. The child can say the number, and then count the objects to see if he was correct.